The Complete

Australia

Travel Guide

2023 & Beyond

A Comprehensive Guide and Tourist Information to Explore Australia Like a Pro

Alexander J Collins

Copyright

The Complete
Australia
Travel Guide
2023 & Beyond

INTRODUCTION

Welcome To Australia

An adventure of a lifetime can be had by visiting Australia. The nation's breathtaking scenery, energetic towns, and distinctive wildlife lure tourists from all over the world. But without a guide, this fantasy trip may easily turn into a nightmare.

Imagine yourself arriving in Australia full of expectation and excitement, only to be swiftly overcome by the amount of information you need to manage. It could be difficult for you to comprehend local customs, locate acceptable lodging, or figure out how to get around. Even some of the most famous tourist destinations in the nation would pass you by if you didn't know they were there.

But don't worry; our travel guide is here to assist you. We are here to guide every of your steps in your Australian experience with our expert advice and insider knowledge. We'll give you important travel information, such as visa requirements, available currencies, modes of transportation, and weather patterns. In-depth guides to some of Australia's most well-known locations, including Sydney, Melbourne, the Great Barrier Reef, and the Australian Outback, will also be provided.

Traveling with confidence will enable you to completely experience Australia's culture and natural beauty, which is the goal of our guide. With our suggestions, you'll be able to explore the nation's distinctive landscapes, find its undiscovered beauties, and make priceless memories. Use our travel guide as your go-to resource for your Australian experience instead of leaving it up to chance.

Welcome to Australia, a place with countless opportunities and stunning natural beauty. Australia is a country that has long captivated travelers' hearts because of its dynamic cities, breathtaking coastline, huge outback, and distinctive fauna.

Our travel guide contains everything you need, whether you want to discover Sydney's famous sites, delve deep into Melbourne's cultural scene, or take in the untamed beauty of the Australian Outback. Our book is filled with insider information, professional advice, and detailed details on everything from lodging choices and transportation alternatives to regional customs and weather patterns, all to assist you in planning your ideal Australian experience.

Everyone can find something to enjoy in Australia, from adventurers and environment lovers to foodies and culture vultures. And with the help of our guide, you'll be able to take advantage of everything that this amazing place has to offer. Whether you're a seasoned tourist or a first-time visitor, this guide is your best tool for learning about Australia's varied landscapes, distinct culture, and enduring landmarks.

So get ready to start your lifelong experience. Your pass to exploring Australia's splendor, thrill, and wonder is our guide. Jump right in, and let's explore!

A Brief History of Australia

Australia has a lengthy, intricate past that dates back thousands of years. Before European explorers came to Australia in the 17th century, indigenous peoples had lived there for over 60,000 years. With the construction of colonies and the eventual creation of the modern nation of Australia, European settlers in the 18th and 19th centuries opened a new chapter in the history of Australia. This essay will examine Australia's history from its Indigenous origins to the present.

Indigenous Australians

Indigenous Australians are thought to have landed in Australia for the first time some 60,000 years ago, and the legacy of their rich culture can still be seen today. Indigenous peoples lived in close connection with the land before the coming of European settlers, engaging in intricate spiritual practices as well as hunting and gathering food from the bush. Before the arrival of the Europeans, the indigenous population of Australia was thought to have been between 750.000 and 1,000,000.

The arrival of Europeans

Willem Janszoon, a Dutch navigator, made the first known European contact with Australia in 1606 while sailing along its northern shore. The eastern coast of Australia was not claimed by Britain until 1770 by British explorer Captain James Cook. British interest in the continent began with Cook's arrival, and the first British colony in Australia was established in Sydney Cove in 1788 with the arrival of the First Fleet.

The early colonial period

Early colonial Australia was characterized by strife between Indigenous Australians and British immigrants. By the middle of the 19th century, the Indigenous population had greatly decreased due to disease, eviction, and violence brought about by the entrance of British colonists. Early colonial times were characterized by conflict with indigenous peoples, as well as the growth of agriculture and industry and the foundation of organizations like schools and churches.

The gold rush era

Australia experienced a huge period of economic prosperity following the 1850s gold discovery. Many immigrants from China were among the many nationalities who arrived during the gold rush in search of their fortunes. The construction of railroads, which helped connect Australia's isolated regions and fueled the expansion of the national economy, was another result of the gold rush.

Federation and the Formation of modern Australia

The movement for federation and the creation of a single Australian nation dominated the late 19th and early 20th centuries. In 1901, the six colonies that had been founded in the 18th and 19th centuries were united to become the Commonwealth of Australia. Australia became noted for its progressive policies, such as women's suffrage and the construction of a social welfare system, and this period of time was characterized by optimism and hope for the future.

World War I and II

Australia's participation in both World Wars had a profound effect on the nation, both socially and economically. Australian soldiers served in the trenches of Europe during World War I alongside British forces, and as a result, the nation saw tremendous social and economic transformation. The country's first national airline, Qantas, was founded during the post-war boom in industry.

Australia participated actively in the Pacific theater of World War II, sending troops there to engage the Japanese in conflicts like the Kokoda Track campaign. The conflict had a huge impact on the nation and signaled the start of a time when Australia's social and political climate underwent significant change.

Post-war period and modern Australia

Australia saw tremendous post-war expansion and development, with an emphasis on industry and infrastructure. Manufacturing in the nation saw a boom, while the building of significant infrastructure initiatives like the Snowy Mountains Hydro-Electric Scheme fueled the economic expansion. Significant social developments in Australian society during the post-war era included the implementation of multiculturalism and the foundation of universal healthcare.

Australia's economy shifted toward services and information technology in the second part of the 20th century, increasing its level of integration with the global economy. Significant social and cultural developments also occurred in the nation, such as the advent of feminism and the development of a powerful Indigenous rights movement.

Australia is a diverse, multicultural country today with a long and complicated past. The nation is renowned for its stunning natural features, which include its expansive deserts, immaculate beaches, and rough coastlines. Many Indigenous Australians are attempting to conserve their cultural history and develop a broader awareness of their contributions to

Australian society. The Indigenous culture of Australia is also appreciated and honored.

Australia's history is a rich and intricate fabric that dates back tens of thousands of years. Throughout its history, Australia has seen enormous changes and alterations, from its Indigenous roots through the introduction of European explorers and the creation of contemporary Australia. Australia is a vibrant, dynamic country today with a deep cultural history and a promising future.

Chapter 1: Essential Travel Information

Currency and Money Matters

The dollar is one of many official currency units used by a number of nations, including Australia. However, Australian dollars are distinct from other currencies in a number of aspects, including their design, their history, and their rate of exchange.

It's beneficial to learn the Australian currency and how to use the country's financial system whether you're moving there or just visiting. Here is our guide on Australian currency, which covers topics such as how to send money to Australia, how to make purchases, and more.

The History of Australian Currency

On the Australian continent, people have existed for tens of thousands of years. The Royal Australian Mint asserts that native currencies were based on a barter system in which tools, shells, and other commodities were exchanged for provisions and food.

In 1788, Europeans founded the first colony in Australia, bringing with them their own money, such as the Spanish dollar and the British pound. But because there wasn't enough money to go around due to the ongoing wars in Europe, rum "became a de-facto currency," according to historian Matt Murphy.

After a while, each state began issuing its own legal currency, such as gold sovereigns, treasury notes, and various coins and banknotes.

The Commonwealth Treasury was established by the federal government in 1901 when Australia became a federation, to handle currency issuance. Similar to the British pound sterling that served as its model, the initial Australian currency was composed of pounds, shillings, and pence.

The Australian dollar, which is divided into 100 cents like the U.S. and New Zealand dollars, took the place of the pound in 1966.

Australian currency denominations

The Royal Australian Mint in Canberra produces coins for the Reserve Bank of Australia (RBA), and Note Printing Australia produces banknotes.

Australian coins are available in six different denominations: $5, $10, $20, $50, $1, and $2. Smaller quantities, such as 1- and 2-cent coins, are uncommon.

There are $5, $10, $20, $50, and $100 banknotes available as paper money, with the most recent iterations having been released between 2016 and 2020.

Six memorable facts about the Australian dollar

Australian money stands out from other dollar currencies due to its vivid banknotes and distinctive coins. On your preferred currency converter, you can recognize it by the letters AUD even though it has the similar symbol as the US dollar.

Here are six other characteristics of the Australian dollar.

1. Australia's currency features British royalty.

Since Australia is a member of the British Commonwealth, the British monarch is considered to be its "head of state." With the late Queen Elizabeth II portrayed on several coins and banknotes, Australia recognizes this in its money. In 2023, new coins bearing the image of King Charles III will be released.

2. The Australian dollar could have been referred to as the "koala."

In 1966, Australia's central bank "decimalized" its currency, replacing the pound and shilling with a far more straightforward decimal system.

However, the moniker "dollar" wasn't a lock. While the public recommended "dinkum," "roo," "kanga," and "koala," the prime minister wanted to call it the "royal."

Ultimately, the "dollar" prevailed, and ever since, the Australian dollar, or "Aussie dollar" as locals refer to it, has been accepted as legal cash.

3. A number of other nations use the AUD as their official currency.

You will need to exchange your Australian dollars for the local currency if you travel to Singapore or New Zealand, two other nations that use the dollar.

However, a small number of nations recognize the Australian dollar as legal money. While Tuvalu and Kiribati have their own currencies that are used alongside the AUD and are tied to it, Nauru utilizes the Australian dollar as its legal unit of exchange.

A number of foreign territories, notably Norfolk Island, the Cocos (Keeling) Islands, and Christmas Island, also utilize the Australian dollar.

Additionally, it served as Papua New Guinea's and the Solomon Islands' official currency for a number of years in the 1960s and 1970s.

4. Australia issued the first polymer banknotes in history.

When it comes to the reliability and security of its currency, Australia is at the top of the list. In 1988, it became the first nation to introduce polymer banknotes, which are more hygienic and durable than conventional paper banknotes.

To stop fraud and counterfeiting, they also have cutting-edge security features like fluorescent ink, microprint, and other characteristics.

5. The sixth-most traded currency is the Australian dollar.

After the euro (EUR), the US dollar (USD), the British pound (GBP), the Japanese yen (JPY), and the Chinese yuan (CNY), the Australian dollar (AUD) was the sixth most traded currency in 2022. It made up 6% of all transactions involving foreign exchange.

6. *Australia has a high-tech banking sector.*

With its largest banks connected through the rapid payment system Osko, Australia boasts one of the most sophisticated financial networks in the world.

Its financial hub is located in Sydney, closely followed by Melbourne. In terms of financial centers worldwide in 2022, Sydney came in at number 13 and Melbourne at number 31.

Additionally, the nation is home to over 775 fintech businesses creating innovative solutions for lending, insurance, and personal finance.

How to pay for goods and services in Australia

You should become familiar with Australian currency if you intend to move to Australia permanently or if you plan to apply for a temporary work visa.

Fortunately, opening a bank account and sending money to and from Australia are simple processes. You are not required to provide traveler's checks. In fact, you might discover that they are more expensive and difficult to cash than other options.

Most establishments in Australia accept debit and credit cards, and ATMs can be found in all major cities and even rural villages.

You may wish to use an ATM to get cash or open a local bank account rather than paying fees on every purchase if you're using a credit or debit card from another country, as your bank may charge costs for international transactions.

You can open a free account with any of the major banks in Australia, such as National Australia Bank, or select a "neobank" that only operates online and has built-in budgeting features.

You don't need to carry around a lot of cash when it comes to hard currency. Tipping is not something people do often in Australia, and even tiny sellers will take purchases made with a credit card or electronic wallet.

Australian currency exchange rates

It's wise to monitor the Australian dollar exchange rate whether you're a resident or a visitor. Be prepared for items to cost more than they do in your own country because Australia has a high cost of living.

Although the Australian dollar is a stable unit of exchange, over time, its value may change due to changes in interest rates, commodity prices, exports, monetary policy, and other variables.

The Australian dollar is typically weaker than the New Zealand dollar and slightly stronger than the US currency.

To check the current exchange rate between 1 AUD and your local currency, use a currency converter. When the AUD is strong, utilize an app for international money transfers like Remitly to send money home to receive the greatest exchange rates.

Weather and Climate

People frequently believe that Australia has perpetual summer or extreme heat. While it is true that Australia has a warm climate in some areas, not all towns or regions experience this. For instance, did you know that Australia is home to a number of excellent ski resorts?

Australia, which is in the southern hemisphere, experiences four distinct seasons: summer (December to March), autumn (March to May), winter (June to August), and spring (September to November). Summer lasts from December to March (with an average temperature of 29°C). While winter is chilly, damp, and windy, summer is scorching and dry. Comparatively speaking to winters in North America or Europe, it is actually a pretty mild winter.

The majority of Australia has four distinct seasons, with the exception of the north, which has just two—a rainy season and a dry season—due to its tropical environment.

The majority of Australia's land is desert, and its climate is semiarid. In actuality, Australia is among the driest nations on earth. The outback, often known as the sand dunes and semi-arid areas that make up 40% of its territory is a unique characteristic of Australia's terrain.

Australia's Climate on the East Coast

Weather in Sydney

The winters in Sydney are particularly warm, with average highs of 24°C in January and 13°C in July. The city receives a reasonable quantity of rainfall that is evenly distributed throughout the seasons, with autumn being the rainiest. Sydney has fair amounts of sunshine, and there can even be sunny days in the winter.

Weather in Brisbane

Brisbane has a hot, muggy, and rainy summer but perfect, brief, and cold winters. With temperatures ranging from 25°C to 30°C, it is a fairly sunny city. There's a reason the region is known as the Sunshine Coast.

Weather in Melbourne

The weather in Melbourne is notoriously unpredictable. The possibility of experiencing all four seasons in a single day is one of its key advantages. The typical summertime temperature ranges from 14°C to 25°C. Melbourne experiences dry summers with sporadic heat waves that can linger for up to three days. The two months of January and February often see Melbourne's highest temperatures, with average highs that occasionally reach 30°C.

Although there may be extended periods of light winds toward the conclusion of the season, fall is characterized by colder temperatures and sunny days. Victoria's northeast, referred to as the High Country, has snowfall in winter when temperatures typically vary from 6.5°C to 14°C. The weather is frequently chilly and gloomy, and frost can form at night. At this time of year, it doesn't often rain heavily. The springtime ranges in temperature from 9°C to 19°C. The weather can change quickly during this season, which is regarded as the most unpredictable of the year.

Climate in Western Australia

Perth is recognized as being the sunniest capital city in Australia, with 131 incredible days of clear skies per year. Perth is ideal for those who love the outdoors, with summer highs averaging 29°C (February being the warmest month) and winter lows averaging 12°C. Perth's weather will allow you to spend a lot of time outside and on adventures.

Summer days at Margaret River and the South West are pleasant (25–35°C), perfect for lounging on the beach and surfing. You can appreciate the views and vineyards in the winter (8-16°C). Temperatures range from 15°C in the winter to 37°C in the summer if you travel farther north to the Esperance region and the Golden Outback. The huge territory has a wide range of climates, yet no matter the conditions, there is always an adventure to be had.

Best Food and Drink Options in Australia

When visiting Australia, be sure to sample these delicious meals! You should definitely try every meal listed below if you have the time because Australian cuisine is really diverse. You'll adore them all, I'm certain of it!

Which one of the many amazing Australian cuisines will you choose as your favorite? Read this page to learn about the most well-known and popular delicacies from the kangaroo's native Australia! Find out immediately what they are!

31

Australian Food

Australia's Most Spectacular Meat and Poultry Dishes

When you visit Australia, you can discover some of the strangest kinds of meat, but they just might become your favorite meat meal! Don't be hesitant to sample one; you'll be pleased with the flavor!

1. Kangaroo Meat

You might be curious as to why Australians consume their national animal. You should be aware that kangaroo is just as juicy and delicious as any other meat you have ever eaten! The major protein source for native Australians is now kangaroo.

Particularly lean red meat: kangaroo meat. You won't need to be concerned about calories when eating it because it has a very low-fat content. Kangaroo meat is treated similarly to other meats by Australians, who can marinade, sauté, or even turn it into a steak if they so choose.

Despite the widespread misconception that kangaroos cannot be consumed, this meat is actually rather common in Australia. You'll be delighted if you try this wonderful and typical kangaroo dish!

Although it may seem strange, kangaroo meat is tasty and worth trying!

2. Crocodile Meat

Australia has crocodile flesh available everywhere! Crocodiles were once solely hunted by the people for their skin, which was used to create leather goods, but thanks to the advancement of Australian cuisine, this white meat has gained enormous popularity there.

Many crocodile meat parts, including steaks and ribs, are used in Australia to create delectable dishes. Cooking crocodiles by marinating the flesh in citrus-based seasonings and frying it in a pan is one of the most popular methods.

3. Emu Meat

The emu, the largest native bird of Australia, must be familiar to you if you've ever looked up food names that start with the letter E.

Everywhere on the country's mainland are emus. It could serve as a source of protein in Australian dishes that resemble beef or lamb. The emu contains red meat, in contrast to other poultry species.

Emu can be prepared in several various ways by Australians. They can roast it in a slow cooker for a delectable breakfast, turn it into steaks, or wrap it in burger buns to produce the ideal burger. In Australia, there is also a kind of meatloaf made using ground emu rather than beef.

4. Barbecue Snag (Thick Australian Sausage)

Australian sausages called "Barbecue Snag" can be made using beef, pork, or mutton. These sausages are probably served in Australia with grilled onions, sauces (tomato, mustard, BBQ sauce, etc.), and a hot dog bun.

Typically, Barbecue Snag can be seen at a sausage sizzle, an Australian and New Zealand tradition. Usually, they raise money for this significant event by selling these snags. Since the 1980s, the Barbecue Snag has also been referred to as a "sausage sizzle."

5. *Chicken Parmigiana*

A chicken meal called chicken Parmigiana, often known as chicken Parmesan consists of breaded chicken breast that is then covered in cheese and tomato sauce. Its name may differ depending on the area in Australia. The three most popular spelling changes are "Parmi," "Parma," and "Parmy."

This dish is American in origin, and it is actually well-liked in American areas with sizable Italian immigrant populations (New Jersey, New York, etc.).

As a standard of Australian pub fare, Chicken Parmigiana can be ordered paired with a drink of beer. It is the ideal option for a filling Wednesday dinner. As a side dish under or adjacent to the main dishes, the locals will often offer Chicken Parmigiana with chips and salad.

6. Carpetbag Steak

A tasty dish called "Carpetbag Steak" combines beef and oysters with butter and garlic. Australia and New Zealand are big fans of this cuisine. It astonishingly became a superstar dish in many nations, especially in the 1950s and 1960s!

The origin of Carpetbag Steak is the British fishing community of Mumbles in South Wales. The most recent Australian variation involves wrapping a prime-cut beef steak with fresh oysters before grilling them whole. The chef will then pour some Worcestershire sauce on top and serve it.

Australian Fish and Seafood at Its Finest

Take a look at the subsequent fish or seafood dishes if you're looking for a more energizing dinner among the tens of thousands of Australian dinner recipes! You should put their names on your list of foods to eat when you visit the kangaroos' native land again.

7. Sydney Rock Oyster

The Sydney Rock Oyster is a unique oyster species that can only be found in Australia and New Zealand. Its scientific name is Saccostrea Glomerata. Because of its stunning look and enduring sweetness, it is referred to as the "jewels of the ocean." Freshly shucked is when it tastes the best.

Sydney Rock Oyster is always eaten raw in Australia with a squeeze of lime or vinegar. It can be prepared by battering it with flour and sautéing it over low heat. Enjoy a glass of Sémillon wine with the oysters! They were meant to be together!

8. Moreton Bay Bug

The coastal crustacean known as the Moreton Bay Bug has a long, narrow tail and a huge, flat head. It is also known as Bay Lobster or Flathead Lobster, and at first glance, you might mistake it for lobster. In Australia, people love to eat fish.

Typically, the flesh in the Moreton Bay Bug's tail is the component that can be eaten. The chef will freeze them for roughly 45 minutes before using them to poach, grill, steam, deep fry, stir-fry, and make a variety of other soups, casseroles, and curries.

9. Prawn Cocktail

In Australia, a prawn cocktail is a traditional seafood dish served at gatherings. It is served in a glass with cocktail sauce and boiling prawns. The unique dipping sauce is made comprised of a horseradish, mayonnaise, and ketchup blend.

The history of the prawn cocktail can be traced back to a California miner who invented an oyster-in-a-glass dish in the 19th century. From the 1960s to the 1980s, this dish was a rising star, and it has maintained that status ever since.

10. Fish' N Chips

Fish N Chips essentially consist of fried fish in batter and French fries, as the name implies. It was first a famous British dish before becoming well-known all over the world. Athanasias Comino, a Greek immigrant, launched the first restaurant serving fish and chips in 1879.

There are currently about 4000 Fish' N Chips restaurants in Australia. On the menus of the majority of bars and restaurants in this country, it is also a pretty well-known name. The "Fish" component of this dish is typically made by Australians using a catfish from the Mekong Delta known as Basa.

11. Barramundi

A multipurpose fish that is indigenous to Australia and the Indo-Pacific is called barramundi, commonly known as Asian sea bass. It is a catadromous fish belonging to the family Latidae. Despite having few calories, barramundi is high in Omega-3 fatty acids and lean protein.

Australia consumes so much barramundi that it is forced to import the fish, which unintentionally puts pressure on local farmers and fishermen. The former listed Fish 'N Chips are also made by the locals using barramundi.

The best examples of Australian cuisine may be found in takeout and convenience foods, which are popular throughout Australia. You can choose these delights from among the tens of thousands of Australian lunch recipes and cuisines for your dinner! Enjoy the finest lunch ever with an Assy!

12. Beetroot Burger

A distinctive Australian burger called the Beetroot Burger comes with a variety of toppings, including blue cheese, fried eggs, avocado, pineapple, grilled onions, and, of course, purple slices of beetroot. Beetroot-topped hamburgers reached their height of appeal in Australia in the middle of the 20th century.

There is a well-known vegetarian and vegan version of the Beetroot Burger in addition to the conventional recipe, which calls for meat and bacon. Instead of meat or eggs, this healthful version includes nuts, legumes, common spices, and herbs.

13. Meat Pie

Both Australia and New Zealand enjoy the popular takeout food known as meat pie. The standard version fits in your palm and is manageable in one hand. It boasts a crispy exterior and a luscious interior filled with pork mince, gravy, mushrooms, onions, and cheese.

This delicious pie is so well-known in Australia that people there view it as their national dish! Meat Pie can be found all over the place in our nation, from tiny unbranded shops to enormous branded bakeries and eateries!

14. Sausage Roll

The ideal way to start a new day is with a sausage roll, one of several Australian breakfast dishes! To make palm-sized buns, the cook will wrap fresh sausages made of beef or pig in a flaky dough cover before placing them all in an oven to bake.

Aussie will sell sausage rolls with unusual sauces like kewpie mayonnaise or barbeque dipping sauce. Your kids can eat it as a handy lunch or snack during recess at school! Children in Australia love sausage rolls as well!

15. Chiko Roll

Another common savory snack in Australia is the chiko roll. To create this cuisine, the locals are influenced by Chinese spring rolls. Typically, the pastry is made of flour, and the inside is composed primarily of barley and cabbage, carrot, meat, celery, and wheat cereal.

Ingenious paper packaging for Chiko Roll was created by Australians so that fans could handle it with ease at football games. It has grown to be a hugely popular fast food takeout option across the nation and even an important Australian cultural symbol!

Chiko Roll has a close connection to Australian surf culture. After a long day of surfing, people sell it at fish and chip stands or corner kiosks by the beach for surfers to enjoy!

16. *Halal Snack Pack*

Doner kebabs made with halal meat (chicken, beef, or lamb) are included in the Halal Snack Pack, along with French fries seasoned with chili, garlic, and barbecue sauce. On occasion, Australians will top the dish with cheese, yogurt, tabbouleh, and jalapenos.

The Halal Snack Pack can be found on most menus in Australia under the abbreviations "snack box," "snack pack," "HSP," or "mixed plate." Its beginnings can be found in Australia in the 1980s. In Adelaide, the "AB" meal using gyro meat is a well-liked variant.

17. *Continental Roll*

Another common sandwich in Australian cuisine that borrows from Italian sandwiches is the Continental Roll or Conti Roll. People will stuff the bread roll with cheese, dried tomatoes, pickled eggplant, beets, carrots, and mixed meat (salami, mortadella, and coppa).

Since the locals typically offer Continental Roll at lunch bars and delis, you might not find it there. When The ReStore in Perth, Western Australia, opened in 1936, it was where it first made an appearance in Australia. As soon as Di Chiera Brothers sold it in 1957, it began to become well-known.

18. *Dagwood Dog*

The hot dog sausage on a stick known as a "Dagwood Dog" originated in Australia. The sausage is typically dipped in a batter made of corn or wheat before being deep-fried in hot oil by the locals. Ketchup will thereafter be provided as a dipping sauce with this hot dog.

The Dagwood Dog is a dish that is American in origin. Dagwood Dog can also be seen in Australia going by the names "Pluto Pup" or "Dippy Dog." The name may change depending on the local circumstances. Do not confuse Dagwood Dog with Battered Savv!

19. Fritz And Sauce

The only ingredients in the traditional Australian sandwich known as Fritz and Sauce are white bread, Fritz, and a small amount of tomato sauce. Kids in Australia love eating it during lunch at school! Additionally, the German settlers group enjoys eating it frequently.

Fritz is where the solution is. Fritz is a sausage made with beef, hog, and lamb scraps together with flour, starch, and seasonings. Other regional names for Fritz include "Devon" in Victoria, "Queensland," "New South Wales," or "Polony" in Western Australia, among others.

20. Dim Sim

Australians call them "Dim Sim," which are similar to Chinese dim Sum but are deep-fried rather than steamed. Another significant variation is in size. Dim Sum is substantially smaller than Dim Sim, which is the size of half a hand. It is yet another Aussie favorite portable snack!

Typically, minced pork, cabbage, and common spices make up the stuffing of a dim sum. The cook will roll the filling into either rectangular or circular shapes after covering it with a dumpling wrapper. Additionally, a carrot, vermicelli, and cabbage-only vegetarian version is available.

In the 1800s, Australians used to offer the mutton variant of Dim Sim to the gold miners. After that, this meal became so well-known thanks to a Chinese immigrant in Melbourne and an Australian celebrity chef.

The Best Australian Desserts with Sweet Pastries

Are you seeking the best desserts from Australia to complete your ideal meal?
Here are some of the top sweet treats and sweets you must try at least once in your life. These foods won't let you down if you have a sweet craving, I assure you!

21. Pavlova

In Australia and New Zealand, Pavlova is a well-known dessert. Australians prepare an egg white Pavlova mixture and bake it slowly to get a crisp crust. The baked good will then be topped by the chef with whipped cream and a selection of delectable Australian fruits, the majority of which are berries.

It bears Anna Pavlova's name, a celebrated Russian ballerina. Before the 1920s, when it was used to commemorate the dancer's tours of Australia and New Zealand, it was initially just a straightforward cream cake without an official name.

During the summer or on rare occasions, Pavlova may be seen in Australia, particularly on Christmas Day. But you can always find it year-round at numerous stores and bakeries around the nation.

22. Lamington

A square sponge cake or butter cake called a lamington has a layer of desiccated coconut on top and is covered with chocolate sauce. It is regarded as the national dessert of Australia. Between the layers of cake in the classic Lamington, there is cream or strawberry jam filling.

Similar to Pavlova, Lamington was given its name in the closing decades of the 19th century in honor of Lord

Lamington, the Governor of Queensland. It is now a famous dessert in Australia, and on July 21, every year, the country celebrates National Lamington Day.

23. Hot Jam Donut

One of Australia's most popular desserts is the Hot Jam Donut, which is especially popular in Victoria. It is available in markets, food festivals, and food trucks. Actually, it is a more yeast-heavy version of the jelly doughnut from America and Germany.

Naturally, Australians would always offer the Hot Jam Donut hot or so warm that, if you're not careful, it could burn your mouth. In Australia, you can also savor this delicious sweet pastry with a cup of coffee or tea.

24. Iced VoVo

An iconic feature of the Australian cookie known as Iced VoVo is a red strip of raspberry jam and two pink strips of fondant icing. Australians use wheat flour and sprinkle shredded coconut on top. It comes from a 1906 trademark application for Arnott's.

In his victory speech after winning the election in 2007, Australian Prime Minister Kevin Rudd made reference to Iced VoVo. The sweet delicacy became so well-known as a result of this occasion that sales of Iced VoVo significantly increased that year!

25. Pikelet

Pikelets are essentially pancakes made in Australia; however, they are significantly thicker and smaller than the French-inspired originals.

The ingredients for pikelets, including baking powder, milk, eggs, sugar, and self-raising flour, are quite similar to those for American pancakes. The batter for pikelets is a little thicker than that of an American pancake. As a result, it gets heavier when it rises on the pan.

Pikelet toppings can also be as simple as jam, fruit, whipped cream, syrup, sugar, chocolate sauce, or whatever you choose. Pikelet is a favorite morning or afternoon tea food in Australia.

The Most Enticed Australian Drinks You Must Sample!

"The Land Down Under" not only boasts the best-tasting food ever, but it also has its fair share of delicious Australian drinks.

Canadian Wine

Are you aware that Australia is one of the major wine exporters? The economy of Australia benefits greatly from the Australian wine industry. Australia is home to thousands of vineyards, many of which are situated in Victoria, Tasmania, New South Wales, etc.

Do you want to know the top Australian wine varieties? Shiraz, Chardonnay, Merlot, Cabernet Sauvignon, Sauvignon Blanc, and Riesling are the most notable wine names. The grape variety from which they are made is often the name given to them.

A glass of wine is a particularly excellent and "Aussie" idea to have after a large lunch.

1. *Flat White Coffee*

The most well-known local coffee beverage in Australia is flat white. It contains espresso and microfoam, which is steamed milk. The barista will apply silky and foamy milk to the top surface to adorn it.

Flat white has less effervescent and airy foam on top than Cappuccino or Latte, which is why some people might confuse it with those beverages. The Flat White was created in the 1980s, although it's unclear where it came from since New Zealand also claims credit for its invention.

2. Milo

Australian children's favorite beverage is unquestionably Milo. It is a malted powder that tastes like chocolate. This product is sold all over the world by Nestlé, a well-known beverage company.

Although Milo is significantly sweeter than cocoa powder, they are similar. You may include the chocolaty powder in a variety of delectable sweet delights in addition to consuming it straight up. For instance, the great Colombian dish Postre de Milo blends pudding and Milo.

Australian chemist Thomas Mayne, who was employed by Nestlé, invented Milo in 1934. At the Sydney Royal Easter Show, the business gave its initial public debut. This beverage attempts to give kids the nutrients they need to grow up healthy.

Nothing beats experiencing what the locals eat and drink in their nation when you are a traveler! With the above list, I hope you've learned more about Australian cuisine and its unique delights.

53

Chapter 2: Transportation Options in Australia

It should not be surprising that traveling across Australia, which covers over 7 million square kilometers (2,968,000 square miles), takes a long time. Given the distances, it seems sense that few people choose to visit the entire nation; there is simply too much land to explore in a short period of time.

Most people travel the nation by plane or limit their exploration to a specific region. It can be challenging to travel around Australia on a budget because of the great distances and hefty transportation costs, especially if you only have a short amount of time.

The huge 14,500-kilometer (9,000-mile) circuit of Australia, which is driven on primary Highway 1, takes weeks to complete. That is also with few pauses and breaks.

However, you should make plans for at least a month (at the earliest) if you want to stop and visit sights along the road. A reasonable time frame is three to six months.

Seriously. It's a sizable nation!

Many "grey nomads"—retirees traveling in campervans—and backpackers spend that much time—or perhaps longer—exploring this beautiful nation and its many distinct landscapes. It takes roughly three to four days to drive directly from Sydney to Perth.

However, what if you only have a few days? What if you have just a few weeks? How do you behave?

It is feasible to travel to Australia on a tight budget. In reality, if you are prepared, it is highly likely.

No of how long you want to stay in Australia, here are some tips for how to travel cheaply:

Getting Around Cheap By Flying

The easiest and most expensive method to travel throughout Australia is this. Because there is little airline competition in this area, flights remain relatively expensive. While a few smaller airlines fly to remote locations, the majority of the country's destinations are served by Qantas (and its subsidiary Jetstar) and Virgin Australia. Tiger Airways, a low-cost airline, stopped operations in 2020, leaving the nation with limited low-cost flight options. These days, Jetstar is the largest low-cost airline.

A brand-new low-cost carrier named Bonza started flying in January 2023 with the intention of connecting underserved cities in Australia. However, it only has a small number of aircraft at the moment.

Ticket prices are high unless there is a significant promotion because there are so few carriers. For instance, a round-trip ticket from Sydney to Perth costs at least 450 AUD ($300 USD), although it typically costs 650 AUD ($437 USD). The approximate cost of the 90-minute flight from Sydney to Melbourne is 211 AUD ($142 USD).

Two of Australia's largest airlines have the following sample fares on well-traveled routes; all prices are in US dollars:

Route	Business Airfare (AUD)	Economy Airfare (AUD)	Economy Train Fare (AUD)	Economy Drive Fare (AUD)
Melbourne - Cairns	$330	$175	$66	$159

Route	Business Airfare (AUD)	Economy Airfare (AUD)	Economy Train Fare (AUD)	Economy Drive Fare (AUD)
Cairns - Perth	$390	$195	$145	$296
Sydney - Cairns	$286	$180	$66	$163
Sydney - Melbourne	$236	$118	$36	$76
Melbourne - Perth	$389	$195	$158	$316
Sydney - Per	$477	$262	$161	$307

Expect to spend substantially more for your flights if you wait to book!

Basically, I wouldn't fly in Australia. When Australians make the joke that it is less expensive to fly to Bali than to travel inside their own country, they are not really joking. I wouldn't recommend flying unless you can get a great offer or are in haste.

Traveling on a Budget with a Backpacker Bus

There are still a few backpacker buses operating in Australia. These are fantastic options for younger travelers who want to party, have fun, and meet other travelers. Everything is planned out for you, so all you have to do is show up and get ready to have a good time!

The party/backpacker bus known as Magic Bus is ideal for those who want to get rowdy. The tour leaves with 25 backpackers ages 18 to 35 once a month for 3 to 4 weeks of camping, bonfires, nonstop parties, and exploring the nation's national parks.

You must plan your trip appropriately to coincide with the scheduled departure because trips leave from Perth in the north to Broome or in the east to Melbourne. Every journey is different since the itineraries are adjustable and allow riders to vote on where to travel and what to do. To ensure that there is always a diverse group, they make an effort to maintain a balance of 50% males and 50% women, as well as a balance of various nations.

The cost of a trip is approximately $250 AUD ($185 USD) per 1,000 kilometers; however, the cost also depends on the route you follow and the length of your particular voyage.

Visit Road2Adventure on Google for a comparable (though more personal) experience. There is enough room for eight people to live and travel in what is essentially a party hostel on wheels. It's significantly smaller than the Magic Bus, though. If you don't want to spend a month with 20 or more other travelers, there are fun alternatives that conduct cross-country treks on set timetables. There are 12–19 day tours available for 2,195–3,785 AUD per person.

Visit www.sharebus.com.au for a more independent choice. As you "share" the bus with nine other passengers and manage everything yourself, it's not quite a tour. They give you instructions on how to use the tools, give you directions and information, and then send you out. In essence, it's a self-guided camping trip with new companions. It's up to you and your fellow passengers what you decide to do.

Their rentals cost between 569 and 1232 AUD per person and last between 10 and 21 days. Their rentals are offered in the southern half of the country, including Tasmania, from October to April, and in the northern half of the country, from April to October. It's a terrific option for vacationers who value independence, enjoy socializing, and enjoy camping.

Using Trains to Get Around Cheaply

The train system in Australia is an excellent method to explore the nation. Australia may be traversed extensively by rail thanks to city trams, commuter trains, long-distance trains, and trans-continental trains. Their use isn't very common, though. Only two other significant train lines run across the entire nation, one running north to south from Melbourne to Darwin and the other running east to west from Sydney to Perth. Train lines are primarily found on the east coast.

Australia, too has unusually high train fares. For instance, a one-way ticket costs $1,200 AUD ($850 USD) and takes three days to go from Sydney to Perth. I wouldn't recommend taking the train across Australia unless you want to spend a lot of money on a romantic route like the Ghan with your significant other (or just adore trains).

These days, there aren't many options to find inexpensive train tickets, so stay away from this mode of transportation. If you decide to ride the train, be aware that tickets for scenic trains sell out months in advance.

Using Car Sharing to Get Around Cheaply

Make friends, rent a car or campervan, and drive across the nation if you truly want to travel on a budget and save money. In addition to giving you a place to sleep if you rent a campervan, this enables you to split the costs with others. More affordable than any other kind of transportation.

In Australia, ridesharing is really simple. Every hostel has a bulletin board where visitors may advertise their need for transportation, and websites like Gumtree and Couchsurfing have busy ridesharing sections where individuals can hunt for vehicles or drivers. It is really sturdy. I STRONGLY advise using this kind of transportation while in the nation.

Some websites for ridesharing include www.coseats.com and www.shareurride.com.au.

Use www.discovercars.com to find the lowest rates for car rentals.

As an alternative, you might potentially buy an automobile from travelers leaving the nation or locals selling secondhand vehicles. Jucy and other rental services are fairly pricey and should only be used as a last option. Typically, you can find a secondhand car for between $750 and $1,500 (USD) in Australia. Even though it seems pricey, you can split the cost with other people, making it the second-most cost-effective method of transportation!

Cheap Public Transportation Getting Around

The public transport services in every Australian city are dependable and reasonably priced. There are even subway and tram systems in the main cities, including Sydney, Melbourne, Brisbane, Adelaide, and Perth. The most affordable method of city travel is this one. The fares range from 3 to 4 AUD.

Avoid taking taxis; they add up quickly. Uber is available in all of the bigger cities and towns if you do need a private ride. Use that instead; it is far less expensive!

What is the Travel Time Across Australia?

In order to help you plan your travels around the nation, the following distance and trip time maps are provided:

Traveling from Sydney

Route	Distance (km/mi)	Flight Duration (hrs)	Train Duration (hrs)	Drive Duration (hrs)
Sydney - Melbourne (inland)	872 / 542	1.5	11.5	14
Sydney - Darwin	4210 / 2610	4.5	55	72

Route	Distance (km/mi)	Flight Duration (hrs)	Train Duration (hrs)	Drive Duration (hrs)
Sydney - Hobart	1589 / 985	2	27 (ferry)	-
Sydney - Adelaide	1412 / 877	2	23	25
Sydney - Canberra	286 / 177	1	3.5	4
Sydney - Perth	4054 / 2513	5	65	66

Traveling from Canberra

Route	Coach (hrs)	Air (hrs)	Road (km/miles)	Rail (hrs)
Canberra – Melbourne	8	1	648 / 402	8.5

Traveling from Melbourne

Route	Road (km/miles)	Air (hrs)	Coach (hrs)	Rail (hrs)
Melbourne – Devonport	307 / 190	1.25	10 (ferry)	–
Melbourne – Hobart	610 / 378	1.25	15 (ferry)	–
Melbourne – Adelaide	731 / 454	1.25	10	10

Traveling from Adelaide

Route	Road (km/miles)	Air (hrs)	Coach (hrs)	Rail (hrs)
Adelaide – Darwin	3021 / 1873	3.75	43.5	49
Adelaide – Alice Springs	1533 / 952	2	20	25
Adelaide – Perth	2706/ 1680	3.25	–	44
Adelaide – Brisbane	2045 / 1270	2.5	32.5	40

Traveling from Perth

Route	Road (km/miles)	Rail (hrs)	Coach (hrs)	Air (hrs)
Perth – Broome	2225 / 1378	-	35	2.5

Traveling from Darwin

Route	Road (km/miles)	Air (hrs)	Coach (hrs)	Rail (hrs)
Darwin – Kakadu	200 / 124	1	–	–
Darwin – Alice Springs	1489 / 924	2.25	22	24

Traveling from Alice Springs

Route	Road (km/miles)	Air (hrs)	Rail (hrs)	Coach (hrs)
Alice Springs – Uluru	443 / 275	0.5	–	–

Traveling from Cairns

Route	Road (km/miles)	Air (hrs)	Rail (hrs)	Coach (hrs)
Cairns – Darwin	2857 / 1771	2.5	5 days	5 days
Cairns – Brisbane	1716 / 1065	2.25	25	29
Cairns – Sydney	2695 / 1671	3	41	47

Traveling from Brisbane

Route	Road (km/miles)	Air (hrs)	Coach (hrs)	Rail (hrs)
Brisbane – Melbourne	1674 / 1039	2	28.5	27
Brisbane – Sydney	965 / 600	1.5	16	14

When planning a trip to Australia, be sure to set aside money for transportation.

Travel is pricey outside of the congested eastern corridor connecting Melbourne and Brisbane. More money than you anticipate will be spent.

If you make the proper plans, you'll save time, money and have a lot better experience!

Getting Around Cheap By Public Bus

One of the favorite modes of transportation in Australia is this. This will be your least expensive choice on the east coast. Buses are shockingly costly on the west coast. There is little competition and few people traveling up and down that coast. In Western Australia, flying out is frequently simpler and more affordable.

On the other hand, if you book in advance, you can obtain really inexpensive bus tickets on the east coast. The largest firm in Australia is Greyhound, and they occasionally have $1 fares.

Here are some examples of bus fares for well-known Australian routes (prices in USD):

71

Route	Premier Fare (AUD)	Greyhound Fare (AUD)
Brisbane - Byron Bay	$28 Adult	$29 Adult
Brisbane - Gold Coast	$17 Adult	$31 Adult
Cairns - Airlie Beach	$107 Adult	$114 Adult
Gold Coast - Byron Bay	$28 Adult	$29 Adult
Sydney - Melbourne	N/A	$120 Adult
Sydney - Canberra	N/A	$51 Adult
Melbourne - Canberra	N/A	$110 Adult
Darwin - Alice Springs	N/A	$301 Adult

The bus passes offered by Greyhound are numerous. The Whimit Passes—hence the name—offer unlimited travel for

15–365 days and are ideal for sporadic travel. They are available in 15, 30, 60, 90, 120, and 365-day passes, priced between 349 and 749 AUD ($235 and 505 USD).

You can go in any direction along any route, and there are more than 180 stations. It's the most practical choice for someone without a car, and it's also the least expensive.

Chapter 3: Accommodation Options

Hotels and Resorts

All around Australia, there are a ton of fantastic places to stay, from fancy city hotels to warm wilderness lodges and island idylls.

There is a luxurious stay that is ideal for you, whether you want the finest creature comforts while viewing Australia's famous animals, prefer being treated in luxury in a big metropolis, or desire exceptional service on an isolated island.

The top 14 resorts and hotels to stay at while visiting Australia are listed below.

Note: *You can verify all the Bellow Hotels in booking.com*

- ## **PARK HYATT SYDNEY**

Excellent for: Sydney Opera House's uninterrupted views

The Park Hyatt Sydney is a residential-style hotel with an exceptional location on the waterfront in Sydney's famed The Rocks district. From here, you can enjoy spectacular views of Sydney Harbour and the glittering "sails" of the Sydney Opera House in the morning. Even the most modest guest rooms are amply sized, with floor-to-ceiling glass doors leading to private balconies. The Park Hyatt provides the largest guest suite in the city, the two-bedroom Sydney Suite, replete with an outdoor patio, dining table seating eight, and its own sauna.

Take in the breathtaking harbor views from your accommodation, relax by the rooftop pool while overlooking the sea, or leave the lobby and board a water taxi at the Park Hyatt's exclusive wharf for a rock-star excursion to a harbourside fine-dining restaurant.

Hotels • Swimming Pool
Price: From AU$1300

- ## EMIRATES ONE & ONLY WOLGAN VALLEY

Excellent for: Nature immersion within striking distance of Sydney

Emirates One & Only Wolgan Valley, a resort with a focus on conservation, is located in the Greater Blue Mountains Area, which is part of the UNESCO World Heritage Site, about three hours by car (or a short helicopter trip) from Sydney. Take a plunge in your private indoor lap pool in a freestanding stone and wood villa before indulging in a treatment at the resort's tranquil spa.

After you've had time to rest and recover, join a group conservation activity conducted by knowledgeable field guides. You can participate in surveys of the beautiful local wombats as part of the WomSAT research program, help plant saplings to help restore bushland corridors for native animals or go on a nature drive to see lots of kangaroos. Watch the sunset from the resort's enormous homestead in the evening before a wonderful meal at Wolgan Dining Room, its flagship restaurant.

Resorts, Retreat, and Lodges • Swimming Pool
Price: From AU$2170

- ## <u>CAPELLA LODGE</u>

Excellent for an exclusive luxury wilderness escape

East of the mainland, Lord Howe Island is a subtropical natural wonderland that is part of the World Heritage Sites. It has soaring volcanic mountains, lush rainforests, and lovely beaches that are framed by the world's southernmost barrier reef. Only 400 people are permitted on Lord Howe at any given time, so Capella Lodge, the most exclusive resort, is tucked away on the remote southern extremity of this spectacular island.

View the South Pacific Ocean and the twin peaks of Mount Gower and Mount Lidgbird from your suite, the lodge's infinity pool, or while indulging in freshly prepared seasonal fare at Capella Restaurant.

Retreat and Lodges • Swimming Pool
Price: From AU$850

- ## **HYATT HOTEL CANBERRA**

Excellent for an atmospheric stay in Australia's capital

At the opulent Hyatt Hotel Canberra in the center of the nation's capital, which has Art Deco and Australian Colonial architecture and is flanked by well-kept gardens, you may travel back in time. The Hyatt Hotel Canberra, located across the street from Old Parliament House and three minutes' drive from Australian Parliament House, was built in the 1920s as a home away from home for politicians and officials, including a serving Australian prime minister.

Enter a roomy Diplomatic Suite to take in the tranquil views of the hotel's beautiful grounds and then relax in the main bathroom's soaking tub for two, which is lined with Italian marble. Enjoy a delicious high tea in The Tea Lounge, cozy up to an open fire in Speaker's Corner Bar, or sip cocktails outside in The Garden Outdoor Bar on a balmy summer evening.

Hotels • Spa/Sauna
Price: From AU$230

- ## RITZ-CARLTON MELBOURNE

Excellent for: A luxurious stay in one of Australia's top cities

The Ritz-Carlton Melbourne is Australia's tallest hotel, towering above the nearby Melbourne buildings on the upper floors of a recently constructed skyscraper. Take an express elevator to the 80th-floor Sky Lobby to check in while admiring sweeping views of the city. You may choose between the roomy regular rooms and the lavish Ritz-Carlton Suite, which has a penthouse-style bathroom with an extra-large soaking tub and sizable dining and sitting areas.

Watch the city far below come to life while eating breakfast at The Ritz-Carlton Lobby Lounge, toast a fantastic day of sightseeing with a handcrafted cocktail at the hotel's cozy Cameo bar, and then enjoy a meal of seasonal local fare at the hotel's Atria restaurant as you take in the brilliant sunset.

- ## **SAFFIRE FREYCINET**

Excellent for: Indulging in gourmet treats and outdoor pursuits

Saffire Freycinet, one of Australia's most famous luxury lodges, is located northeast of Hobart, just outside the breathtaking Freycinet National Park. Visit one of the 20

rooms spread across the coastal bushland and take in the spellbinding views of Great Oyster Bay and the Hazards Mountains. Then proceed to Saffire's spectacular main lodge, which features an organic design modeled after the shape of a stingray, and find a seat by the restaurant Palate's floor-to-ceiling windows for supper. You can eat degustation dinners here that feature renowned fresh Tasmanian seafood and produce and are complemented with top-notch regional wines.

Set aside a few days for days of intriguing experiences that are included, such as enjoying oysters that have just been harvested from the bay at Freycinet Marine Oyster Farm, seeing Tasmanian devils, or connecting with your native land with an Aboriginal guide. Alternatively, choose iconic activities like a trip to picturesque Wineglass Bay.

Hotels, Resorts, Retreat, and Lodges • Spa/Sauna
Price: From AU$2100

• THE LOUISE

Excellent for: A tranquil getaway in a world-class wine region

When you stay at The Louise, you'll experience a sense of unhurried elegance and have unmatched access to one of Australia's oldest and most prominent wine districts. This upscale retreat is located in the Barossa Valley wine region, a short helicopter ride or hour's drive from Adelaide. It is surrounded by vineyards. Each of The Louise's spacious, Mediterranean villa-style rooms has an outdoor rain shower and an open fireplace, and they also have their own courtyards with views of shiraz grape-planted rows of vines.

Many of the lodge's employees have lived in the area for a long time and have strong ties to the region's winemakers, suppliers, and chefs; take advantage of this knowledge when you eat at the signature restaurant Appellation or the casual diner Contour before venturing out to explore the excellent cellar doors and restaurants dotting the valley.

Hotels, Retreats, and Lodges • Swimming Pool
Price: From AU$1000

- ## SOUTHERN OCEAN LODGE

Excellent for: Appreciating exquisite cuisine and amazing fauna

In the latter half of 2023, Kangaroo Island's Southern Ocean Lodge, a wildlife haven, plans to reopen. The new-look Southern Ocean Lodge has been painstakingly renovated and redesigned by its owners and original architect, with environmental sustainability at its core. The main lodge's 25 guest suites have been repositioned to better make use of the expansive ocean vistas and coastal vegetation, and a new

Ocean Pavilion with four bedrooms is set off from the other structures.

All-inclusive dinners featuring South Australian and Kangaroo Island produce are still available, and you may savor them while taking in the serene scene of waves constantly crashing into the wild Southern Ocean.

Retreat and Lodges • Spa/Sauna
Price: From AU$1250

- ## COMO THE TREASURY

Excellent for: A classy lodging in Perth's downtown

Como The Treasury is a character-filled getaway right in the heart of Perth that is housed among three opulent historic government structures from the 19th century. Kerry Hill, a Perth native who designed the inside of many Aman Resorts, created the hotel's modest, ultra-luxe aesthetic. For a luxurious area with a dining room that seats six people and a bedroom that offers views of the Swan River, reserve the Como Suite, the hotel's largest room type. Alternately, select a Heritage

Balcony Room with big French doors opening to a sandstone balcony with views of the attractive St. Georges Cathedral.

You should book a table at the rooftop fine-dining restaurant Wildflower and treat yourself to a custom massage at the hotel's Como Shambhala Urban Escape. Wildflower bases its meals on the six seasons of the local Noongar Aboriginal calendar.

Hotels • Swimming Pool
Price from AU$665

- ## EL QUESTRO HOMESTEAD

Great for: Reconnecting with nature in a historic wilderness

El Questro Homestead, a 10-suite clifftop resort located within the expansive El Questro Wilderness Park in the Kimberley, is the epitome of bush luxury. The homestead, an oasis of luxury amid one of the roughest wilderness areas, overlooks the tranquil Chamberlain River from the top of a striking burnt-orange cliff. Visit the adults-only homestead's premier suite, the Chamberlain Suite, and enjoy the wraparound verandah while watching the sunset over the gorge. Alternately, reserve a freestanding Cliff Side Retreat and take in the breathtaking views from your feather-topped bed before joining other visitors for a three-course supper with paired wines.

A guided walk through Kimberley's historic wilderness, participation in bird-watching and bush culture tours, a boat along the Chamberlain River, and unique access to the enchanted Zebedee Thermal Springs are all included in your stay.

Resorts, Retreat, and Lodges • Swimming Pool
Price: From AU$2155

- ## **LONGITUDE 131°**

Great for: Connecting in style to the center of the Red Centre

Many tourists have it on their bucket lists to visit the famous monolith Uluru and the enormous domes of Kata Tjuta in Australia's Red Centre. You can observe Uluru's famed color changes as the sun sets from the outdoor lounge of your pavilion at Longitude 131°, a luxurious lodge on the edge of the Uluru-Kata Tjuta National Park in the Northern Territory, or from the comfort of your bed.

From vantage spots across Longitude 131°, such as Dune House, the location of the lodge's restaurant and bar, and the elevated Dune Top platform, located apart from the main lodge, you can also take in uninterrupted views of Uluru and the neighboring Kata Tjuta domes. The Ernabella Arts Centre in the Anangu Pitjantjatjara Yankunytjatjara Lands, whose artists' work is displayed throughout the lodge, is the ideal starting point for the exploration of this historic location.

Retreat and Lodges • Swimming Pool
From AU$1700

- ## <u>QUALIA</u>

Excellent for: Experiencing the Whitsundays in tranquility

It is simple to travel to the opulent resort Qualia because there are direct flights to Hamilton Island in the Whitsundays from some of Australia's major towns. It might be more challenging to persuade your traveling buddy to leave this gorgeous resort. Make yourself at home in a breezy Windward Pavilion, where you may relax on the terrace chaises or in the private plunge pool while admiring the expansive views of the Coral Sea. A spacious, open-plan retreat with sizable living and dining rooms and a separate one-bedroom guesthouse is the private Beach House.

Some of the Great Barrier Reef's most picturesque locations, such as the neighboring Whitehaven Beach, renowned for its snow-white sand, and Heart Reef, are accessible from Qualia via a short scenic flight or a leisurely boat trip.

Hotels, Resorts • Swimming Pool
From AU$1640

• **LIZARD ISLAND**

Excellent for: Enjoying a secluded section of the Great Barrier Reef

Lizard Island is located at the far-northern extremity of the Great Barrier Reef and is accessible through an hour-long charter aircraft from Cairns. Take over the three-bedroom House at Lizard, a magnificent three-floor lodge on a remote peninsula distant from the main resort, or retreat to the cliff-top Villa or the super-private Pavilion. All of these accommodations provide stunning views of the ocean.

Explore the nearby national park's bushland, go snorkeling off one of the island's many beaches, or take your time enjoying a quiet picnic on a private stretch of sand. Get on a boat and travel to the well-known Cod Hole dive site to wonder at the underwater environment, or visit the neighboring Ribbon Reefs to try your hand at big-game fishing.

Resorts, Retreat, and Lodges • Swimming Pool
From AU$1558

• <u>SILKY OAKS LODGE</u>

Excellent for: Releasing stress in a lush rainforest

At the chic Silky Oaks Lodge, situated north of Cairns in the World Heritage-listed Daintree Rainforest, you can reset and rejuvenate. Choose a roomy Billabong Suite with a view of the Mossman River high in the treetops, then relax in the hammock on the patio and lose track of time while listening to the sound of gurgling water and birdcalls. The large covered balcony and inviting infinity pool of the magnificent two-bedroom Daintree Pavilion offer views of the tropical jungle.

Spend idyllic days getting pampered at the Healing Waters Spa and eating delectable tropical cuisine prepared with fresh ingredients right from the lodge's kitchen garden. Join a safari to Cape Tribulation, where the rainforest meets the Great Barrier Reef, to learn about the Traditional Owners' relationship to the rainforest, or go on an Aboriginal-led Dreamtime walk through Daintree National Park's Mossman Gorge.

Retreat and Lodges • Swimming Pool
From AU$480

Budget Hotels In Sydney, Australia

Sydney is not known for having cheap hotels; for the majority of the year, rates are on par with those in London and New York. The main factor is persistently high occupancy rates; year-round, 85% of Sydney's hotels are filled.

In Sydney, a 3-star hotel room often costs $250, while a 5-star hotel room would probably cost you more than $400. It can be doubled if you go during the busy season.

Given this, the cost of a "budget hotel" in this city can range from $120-$190 per night. A private room or small dorm in one of Sydney's top hostels is definitely your best option if you're searching for something more affordable.

How did we decide which cheap hotels in Sydney to include on this list?

The accommodations that made our list had to adhere to a few criteria:

- They have to be conveniently situated near first-rate public transportation options or within easy walking distance of the city center.

- No one wants to go on vacation and sleep in a dirty hotel, no matter how tight their budget, so they had to be clean.

- Additionally, they needed to constantly receive positive online customer service reviews. When client expectations are too high, any budget hotel will occasionally receive a bad review; however, we have only listed locations that receive positive reviews on the whole.

What to anticipate from a low-cost hotel in Sydney

- Older-style houses that have undergone renovations and have the word "boutique" applied to the name

- Elevators are less common than staircases; however some have both
- Some lodgings could have communal restrooms.
- Limited reception hours—most won't have a 24-hour reception.
- Fewer amenities than the big chain hotels—things like gyms and pools are more unusual.
- No on-site dining or room service; nevertheless, many hotels feature a cafe in the same or nearby building.

Some of these properties are wrongly labeled as 3–4 stars as a result of the self-rating methods provided on most hotel booking websites. The majority of cheap lodgings, from experience, are in the 2-3 star level. The cost increases as the stars rise!

A hotel's star rating of 2-3 does not imply that it is subpar. Simply said, it indicates that they provide fewer conveniences to visitors. Setting your expectations is crucial; you want a decent quality-to-price ratio. This may require you to give up certain extras, but if you want to get a cheap hotel in Sydney, you have to do it.

Just a quick word on the guest reviews we publish for each property. These are obtained from Booking.com, and frequently the lower ones (the 7-8s) have been rated that way because of a lack of amenities, as you could anticipate from a low-cost resort. If you look attentively, you will notice that we have left out any properties with poor ratings for personnel and comfort.

When in Sydney, is it tough to get a cheap hotel?

Finding inexpensive hotels in Sydney is difficult. In fact, during the following seasons of the year, any notion of a deal should be abandoned:

Christmas and New Year's, Mardi Gras (February/March), Easter, the Vivid Sydney Festival (May/June), and any long weekend or NSW school vacation.

The times of year when it costs the most to travel to Sydney are these. Before making plans, it's a good idea to review this list of NSW school vacation dates. If you want to visit during these dates, as soon as you can, book your trip, and be prepared to pay more than $350 per night, even at these "budget" hotels.

In order to find properties at lesser prices, it's also a good time to search deeper into the suburbs or think about Airbnb!

Cheap lodging near Sydney Harbour

You might assume that you would be out of luck if your ideal vacation rental included harbor views and a modest price. I'm delighted to say that you can find that, as long as you're content with the views from the rooftop terrace or other public places rather than your bedroom window.

The hotels in this area are either close to the harbor frontage or have views that are available to the general public.

- ## <u>The Russell Hotel – The Rocks</u>

Guest Rating: 9.1/10 | Location: The Rocks

The Russell Hotel is a boutique hotel with a variety of rooms and rates that is conveniently situated in a stunning historic building on George Street at the start of the Rocks.

The beds are quite comfy, the rooms are a reasonable size, and the water pressure in the shower was excellent.

The Museum of Contemporary Art and Circular Quay are direct across the Street, and downstairs there is a tiny pub called The Push that is a wonderful place for a pre-dinner drink. Attributes of the Russell Hotel

- There is no air conditioning, but there are ceiling fans and windows that open
- Although there is an elevator to most levels, it's not truly an accessible hotel.
- Some of the more affordable rooms have communal bathrooms, but ensuite rooms are only a few dollars more.

- Less than 5 minutes' walk will get you to Circular Quay pier and train station from the hotel, albeit there are some stairs to negotiate.

There is wonderful service and immaculate common amenities. It is an excellent option if you can obtain one for a fair price.

Location: Circular Quay

Those on cruises, couples, and singles who want a central location may stay here.

- ## YHA Sydney Harbour

Guest Rating: 9.5/10 | Location: *The Rocks*

Because it's a little unique, this hostel managed to make my list of the top "hotels." The view from this Sydney hostel's roof terrace has to rank among the best hostel vistas in the entire world, and secondly, inexpensive rooms are hard to come by in this area of the city.

The Harbour Bridge is right outside of YHA Sydney Harbour. This sprawling home has 350 bedrooms and is situated on an old settlement. The building was constructed around the artifact ruins that were discovered when excavation got underway.

Watch the sunrise behind the Opera House by getting up early. Features:

- The hostel boasts good amenities, including a spacious kitchen, a games room, and eating areas.
- All rooms, even dorms, have private bathrooms.

101

- The majority of the family and double rooms have flat-screen televisions, and the king and queen rooms also have such.

- The hostel draws people of all ages, including elders and families with young children.

A one-week minimum stay is required on New Year's Eve, and accommodations are typically sold out by March.

Location: 110 Cumberland St, the Rocks

Everyone could stay here! Families of every age, single travelers, and groups of friends traveling together will enjoy the hostel. It's a little bit of a walk from the station, so it might not be the best for people with mobility concerns.

Budget hotels in Sydney's CBD

Budget hotels in Sydney's central business district

The center of town is good in terms of walking accessibility to major landmarks and convenience to shopping, if that's your thing, even though it isn't as picturesque as other parts of the city. Finding a cheap hotel in Sydney's Central Business District could prove to be difficult. Even yet, there are a few accommodations that routinely provide rates below $250 per night, especially on weekends.

- ## **Mercure Martin Place**

Guest Rating: 7.9/10 | Location: *Martin Place*

Macquarie Street and Hyde Park are both about a two-minute walk from Mecure Martin Place.

This hotel, which is only a short distance from St. James or Martin Place stations, was formerly known under the Travelodge name. Even while it won't win any design honors and the surroundings are a little antiseptic, you can walk to almost everything you'll want to see and do, and on weekends the costs are rock bottom.

You will be in a good location to tour Hyde Park and walk along Macquarie Street in history.

Features:

- Each of these large rooms has a tiny kitchenette with a microwave, sink, and kettle.
- They feature modern furnishings
- Triple bedrooms are available

- A coin-operated laundry is present, which is uncommon for Sydney hotels.

There isn't a restaurant or room service on the property; however, there are a lot of eateries around for breakfast. For a great breakfast, visit the charming Jardin St. James at the top of the Street. You can reach Circular Quay and Pitt St Mall in under 10 and 5 minutes, respectively, of walking. Starting at $240 for a night.

Location: Phillip St Sydney

Business travelers, singles, couples, and shoppers could stay here.

- ## **Megaboom City Hotel**

Guest Rating: 8.3/10 | Location: *Town Hall*

The Queen Victoria Building is 3 minutes away on foot, and the harbor is also accessible by foot from Magaboom, making it a convenient starting point for exploring the city. Megaboom gets high points for location because many of Sydney's best little bars are right outside your door, and Pitt Street Mall is nearby.

The rooms are clean and pleasant, despite the drab decor, and are often priced between $125 and 190 per night, making them a decent deal.

Features:

- They offer free high-strength WiFi
- Each room has a refrigerator
- The hotel only has one elevator, so if you are on a higher floor, it may take some time, but you get a nice quiet room in exchange.
- Some visitors claim that the first few floors can hear train rumblings as well. If you have trouble falling asleep, consider booking a room on the upper floor.

In general, this property offers excellent value.

Location: *Level 1 93 York St, Sydney*

Only singles and couples could stay here because the rooms can be on the small side.

- ## **Song Hotel Sydney**

Guest Rating: 7.7/10 | Location: Museum Station

The Song Hotel, formerly the YWCA, is not fancy but is worth considering if money is tight. I advise you to bring earplugs if you are a light sleeper because this hotel is close to a major crossroads that leads up to Kings Cross and is located across from the southern end of Hyde Park.

Aside from Hyde Park lies the Song Hotel.

However, the fact that you are in the midst of the city and can easily walk to Surry Hills, Darlinghurst, and the CBD is a benefit of all that noise. Even Darling Harbour is accessible on foot. There is also plenty of room in the park for children to run around.

- A variety of accommodation sizes, including single, double, and a few rooms that sleep four;
- Several rooms with shared bathrooms to help you save a little extra money.
- The family rooms contain a microwave to aid with meal expenditures.

- You can pay a little more for premium rooms that have just been renovated and have double-glazed windows to reduce street noise.

Take a look at the reviews to determine whether any of the issues mentioned would be of concern to you. If you can find one at a fair price, the upgraded rooms seem to be in demand.

Location: 5-11 Wentworth Avenue

Shoppers and families with older children could stay here.

Darlinghurst, Kings Cross, Potts Point, and Surry Hills's Best Cheap Hotels

There are a lot of tiny boutique hotels in this area of the city, which is located between the central business district and the eastern suburbs. This might be a result of the sheer volume of little apartment complexes that sprung up in this area during the 1930s housing boom in the city. There are several gems among these properties that make it simple to convert them into modest hotels.

Personally, I really like this. It's a great gourmet destination, and all three of these neighborhoods have a village-like atmosphere. You can find charming neighborhoods with

Victorian homes that date back to the colony's rich citizens of the 19th Century among the cafes and tiny taverns.

As the streets lead to the water, there are many beautiful harbor vistas waiting to be discovered.

The city's red light and party district, Kings Cross, may still be included in your guidebook, but the tide has definitely changed. I think this area is safer than some of the streets near Central Train Station.

In spite of the fact that this area was formerly the epicenter of Sydney's underbelly, it has recently gotten a little more somber. If you are easily offended, however, you may still find some areas of Kings Cross to be a touch sleazy.

- ## Hotel Challis

Guest Rating: 8/10 | Location: Potts Point |

One of the oldest buildings in the neighborhood, Hotel Challis is situated on one of Potts Point's most charming lanes. Only a few of the compact doubles here, measuring just 12m2, are within the price range. The beds are quite comfy, and the location couldn't be better. They may only be just big enough to swing a cat.

The staff is frequently complimented for their friendliness. If I could afford the balcony room, I would gladly stay here, and it might be difficult to convince me to check out. You can travel by foot through Wolloomooloo and the Botanic Gardens to enter the city from here.

Check out the Hotel Challis' rates and accommodation options.

Location: 21-23 Challis Avenue, Potts Point,
Couples, Solo travelers, and foodies could stay here

- ## The Jensen

Guest Rating: 8.1/10 | Location: *Potts Point*

The Jensen is a small, welcoming hotel located in a bustling neighborhood 500 meters from Kings Cross train station. The city center may be reached on foot in 25 minutes, and the Botanic Gardens in 15 minutes. The Street is wonderful, and there are many restaurants right outside your door, including the popular Cho Cho San and vegetarian eatery Yellow. A few supermarkets are also close by.

The communal restrooms are clean and handy to your room, despite the fact that the rooms are modest. All rooms have air conditioning, and you can get a room with a balcony.

This is a wonderful option for groups because of the quad or triple rooms.

The absence of an elevator and ensuite bathrooms is a drawback, but I would still stay here at the correct price regardless of these drawbacks.

Location: 71 Macleay Street, Potts Point,

 Due to the size of the rooms, solo and a couple of travelers are best suited to stay here.

- ## No 9 Springfield

Guest Rating: 7.9/10 | Location: Kings Cross Station

Just 240 meters separate No 9 Springfield from Kings Cross station, which is a good value. There is a lot to enjoy about this place, whose costs are often between $130 and 160.

Kings Cross Station is a 2-minute walk from Springfield Lodge.

I'm strongly reminded of inner-city London on this street. There are many excellent restaurants on Victoria Road close by, including The Butler, with its stunning city views, and the popular Asian fusion restaurant Ms. G's.

Features include: opening the old-style windows, which improve airflow; free WiFi for all visitors; refrigerators in each room; an on-site restaurant; and shared laundry facilities.

The staff is helpful, and there are many restaurants in the neighborhood. Although there are single rooms, they are rather small, so even if I were traveling alone, I would definitely pay more for a double.

The address is 9 Springfield Avenue in Potts Point.
Solo travelers, couples, and foodies should stay here.

- ## <u>Sydney Boutique Hotel</u>

Guest Rating: 8.2/10 | Location: Darlinghurst

Sydney Boutique Hotel is a tiny (16 rooms) establishment located near a variety of cafes and restaurants that will keep you occupied in the evenings.

The Kings Cross train station is a 3-minute walk from the hotel, and the 311 bus (which travels from Railway Square via

Wolloomoolloo to Barangaroo) stops right around the corner. In 20 to 25 minutes, you may walk into the city center.

There are two amenities in each room: (1) Free WiFi and (2) Fridges.

Superior accommodations include balconies that are a reasonable size and recently remodeled rooms.

Only single travelers or amicable couples should stay in the "standard" rooms, which range in size from 10 to 22 square meters.

Location: In Darlinghurst, at 114 Darlinghurst Road.

Who ought to remain here: Ideal for single travelers and couples who wish to be close to nightlife, clubs, and cafés. The rooms are very small for a family; therefore I wouldn't suggest it.

There are a few places around where kids can run off some steam.

Best low-cost lodging south of the CBD

We defined the south of the CBD as covering Glebe, Redfern, and Chippendale, as well as the vicinity of Central Station. Some areas of the southern CBD are somewhat unsightly, with a lot of construction sites and dilapidated homes near Central

Station, while other areas, like Chippendale and Surry Hills, have experienced a revival in recent years and are now highly sought-after hipster hotspots.

I advise you to look up any address on Google Maps street view to get a sense of the neighborhood.

- ## **Metro Hotel Marlow Sydney Central**
Guest Rating: 8.2/10 | Location: Darlinghurst

The Metro Marlow is the ideal place for anyone visiting the area to see a play and a delicious dinner because it is only a short distance from Thai Town and the Capitol Theatre. It is well positioned for seeing the entire city and inner suburbs because Central Station is only a 7-minute walk away, and the light rail is only 3 minutes away.

The following amenities are provided:

- There is a small rooftop pool;
- Family rooms are available, and many rooms sleep three;
- The rooms are larger than normal for hotels in Sydney at this price;

- They have 24-hour reception and room service;

Location: Sydney, 431-439 Pitt St.

Travelers seeking the amenities of a chain hotel without the high cost should stay here.

On the North Shore of Sydney Harbour, Cheap Hotels Properties on the north shore, particularly those with simple ferry access, are a beautiful choice if you'd like to escape the bustle of the city.

It resembles taking a vacation while on vacation. Yes, once you've finished exploring the city, it will take you around 20 minutes to return to your hotel. However, you will get the opportunity to experience the harbor lifestyle that only a very select few Sydneysiders are fortunate enough to enjoy.

- **<u>View Sydney</u>**

Guest Rating: 8.4/10 | Location: North Sydney

With a stay at View Sydney, you'll be minutes from North Sydney Station and just a few meters from Harbour's Edge. A budget room at this hotel will provide you with a North Sydney View instead of the hotel's wonderful harbor views; thus, there won't be any glittering harbor vistas from your bedroom window.

The following amenities are available in each of the North Sydney view rooms:

- On-site restaurant and gym;
- A view-oriented outdoor patio area.
- A workstation
- A sizable window with plenty of natural light
- A flat-screen TV, and WiFi

This is a fantastic option, and their harbor view rooms are excellent if you have money to spare. Who knows, you might receive a promotion.

This hotel is fantastic for NYE.

Location: North Sydney, 17 Blue Street

Who should stay here: Anyone looking for a decently sized room only about ten minutes by rail from the city.

- ## **Glenferrie Lodge**

Guest Rating: 8.2/10 | Location: Kirribilli

In the Kirribilli neighborhood of the lower north shore, Glenferrie is a boutique hotel built in a historic structure with plenty of natural light. It is one of Sydney's top-value options, in my opinion.

The location, only a short distance from the water's edge, is the main selling point. The distance between the two ferry wharves is only a short stroll, and it takes only 25 minutes to cross the Sydney Harbour Bridge and enter the city.

Features:

- Tastefully decorated with cozy beds and furniture; air conditioning; and ceiling fans
- A variety of hotel types, including family rooms and tiny singles with shared bathrooms;
- A good buffet breakfast;
- A sizable garden and children's playground

For New Year's Eve in Sydney on a budget, this is also my #1 recommendation!

Location: 12 Carabella Street, Kirribilli
Excellent for both families and lone travelers, this hotel is recommended. This is a great option if you want to be close to the city yet still feel like a (wealthy) local.

- ### **Cremorne Point Manor**

Guest Rating: 8.5/10 | Location: Cremorne

Recent renovations turned this two-story Federation-style estate into a stunning guesthouse/hotel with harbor views that far exceed its asking price. The customer service is great, and the value for the money is difficult to match. Winner of 5 Tripadvisor Excellence Awards.

Just a short stroll from the Manor, Cremorne provided this perspective of the city.

The luxury penthouse, which sleeps five people, is priced at about $120 per person per night, making it a good value in this pricey city. Other features include:

- Full range of rooms from tiny single rooms with shared bathrooms up to a two-bedroom penthouse.
- The location is excellent; it takes only three minutes to walk to the boat, and it takes eight minutes to cross the harbor to go to Circular Quay.
- You are surrounded by lovely waterfront walks, and the adorable Mccullum Pool is only a short distance away. Taronga Zoo is equally accessible on foot.

Advice: This property is not appropriate for anyone with mobility concerns; however, disabled access is accessible with help (lift). Outside of the busiest times, last-minute accommodations are frequently offered at great rates.

Location: Cremorne Point's Cremorne Road
Who should stay here: Anyone seeking a more authentic experience; excellent for both single and family travelers.

Hotels in the Eastern Suburbs

However, we have managed to identify a few that we would consider. The Eastern suburbs of Woollahra and Paddington are home to some substantial affluence and not exactly a place you would expect to find cheap hotel rooms.

- ## **The Hughenden Boutique Hotel**

The 1878-built Victorian home is located in one of Woollahra's most charming streets, with buses to the city and Bondi Beach stopping right outside your door. French Renaissance-style décor might be used to characterize the individually equipped rooms. This hotel is an excellent value for Sydney and has just undergone renovations. It would undoubtedly entice those who enjoy the charm of the past.

There are five dog-friendly rooms with balconies if you're traveling with your pet, as well as a range of accommodations, including compact doubles, queens, kings, suites, spacious family rooms, and deluxe rooms. There are also numerous public seating areas and a small on-site cafe.

Centennial Park, an excellent place for a morning run and to watch wild cockatoos, is only a short distance away.

Location: Woollahra, 14 Queen Street

Travelers with dogs, people who enjoy old-world elegance, and those seeking an upscale, calmer area should stay here.

Budget Hotels by the Beach

Budget and beach don't mix well in Sydney because most hotels there cost more than $200 per night. There are certain exceptions, but you should verify before becoming very excited because they might not always fit the budget!

A beach hotel is definitely the ideal option if you're dreaming of spending some of your Sydney vacations paddling in the ocean or strolling along the sand. If you choose to stay near the shore, Several things should be kept in mind. First of all, it will take you at least 30 minutes to get to the harbor's top sights, and on weekends, these places may get quite loud.

- ## Coogee Sands Hotel

The Coogee Sands is situated immediately next to the Coogee Pavilion, a popular local hangout at the northern end of Coogee Beach. The Bondi walk begins at the front door and is less than 50 meters from the beach. Just a short stroll will get you to Bondi Junction and buses to the city.

The Sands is the structure on the left, and the sizable Coogee Pavilion is a well-liked gathering place for locals.

Features:

- A range of available rooms, some with breathtaking water views
- There are kitchenettes in every room.
- A BBQ sundeck is on Level 6.
- There is a 24-hour reception;
- There is no on-site eating available; however, a number of nearby eateries offer chargeback service.

Advice: *Because of how popular this location is, it can get a little boisterous. If this worries you, ask for a room distant from the Street or bring earplugs.*

Location: *Coogee, 161–167 Dolphin St.*

Who should stay here: *Families should choose this location because there is room to run about right outside the door. Additionally ideal for individuals who like to mix sightseeing with a beach vacation.*

Camping and Caravan Parks

These are Australia's top caravan parks, listed by state.

Many of the caravan parks of today are environmentally friendly, situated on some of the best coastal or inland real estates in the nation, and have amenities that are on the verge of resort-level caliber.

They are not to be laughed at as a cheap travel alternative.

Here are the parks that AT thinks are doing it right.

New South Wales

- **BLUE DOLPHIN HOLIDAY RESORT, YAMBA**

The caravan park in Yamba, which is primarily recognized as a charming fishing village and surf destination, is growing in popularity.

Awesome vistas are provided by Yamba's spectacular location on the Pacific coast.

The Blue Dolphin combines three crucial elements—location, a tranquil ambiance, and kid-friendly activities—and tops most travelers' lists as the ideal caravan park to spend a family vacation.

The Park, which is situated at the mouth of the powerful Clarence River, is surrounded by 15 acres of tropical gardens

122

& is close to an 18-hole golf course, a bowling alley, and seven surfing beaches that enjoy the year-round sunshine of northern New South Wales.

Don't skip: Yamba Prawn sampling.

Information: *Yamba Rd, Yamba (02) 6646 2194, from $30 per night.*

• FIRST SUN CARAVAN PARK, BYRON BAY

Due to its location directly on Byron's major beach and its proximity to Cape Byron, Australia's most easterly point, this vacation park truly benefits from views of the rising sun every morning.

Belongil Beach, Byron Bay, and Bluewater on the Beach.

Since the sites are situated directly on the shoreline of the major beach, there isn't much to hinder the views of its visitors.

Over time, Byron has developed into a Mecca for cool people who enjoy the sun, pleasure, and alternative culture.

You won't miss a beat because our Park is close to all the major attractions.

A leisurely hike to the Lighthouse and its breathtaking views of the South Pacific Ocean are not to be missed.

Information: *Lawson St, Byron Bay, www.bshp.com.au/first, (02) 6685 6544, starting at $50 per night.*

- **HUSKISSON BEACH TOURIST RESORT, JERVIS BAY**

Jervis Bay, which is only two hours south of Sydney, is the ideal destination for a weekend getaway or longer vacation.

One of the numerous stunning nooks with white sand in Jervis Bay

This Park has immaculate amenities and gorgeous surroundings, yet it's far enough away to be relaxing. However, if you get bored of lounging in the crystal clear waters or exploring parklands, you do have other options: this caravan park is close to specialty shops, restaurants, cafes, the neighborhood pub, and much, much more, and it is only a short stroll from the town of "Husky."

Visit Hyams Beach, which is thought to have the whitest sand on earth.

Information: Beach St., Huskisson, 1300 733 027, from $35 per night.

Western Australia

- ## ESPERANCE SEAFRONT CARAVAN PARK

Esperance's beaches are regarded as some of the best in the world, and they are home to some of Australia's most beautiful coastline.

Every site at the Esperance Seafront Caravan Park has a view of the ocean, and it is only two kilometers from the town center and 50 meters from a safe swimming beach. Ideal for exploring Cape Le Grand's untamed national parks, the neighboring pink lake, and the Bay of Isles' cobalt blue water.

The local sea lion that resides under the nearby fishing jetty is a sight not to be missed.

Details: *Goldfields Road, Esperance, (08) 9071 1251, from $26 per night.*

- ## MONKEY MIA DOLPHIN RESORT CAMPING

Swimming with dolphins is something that everyone wants to do.

The Monkey Mia Dolphin Resort provides a free human-dolphin contact program. Monkey Mia is one of the few places in Australia where dolphin visits are daily rather than seasonal.

This camping facility is directly on the beach and is located in the Shark Bay World Heritage Area.

Don't miss An Aboriginal Cultural Walk, a camel ride, or snorkeling or boating in pristine waterways.

Details: *(08) 9948 1320, $31 per night.*

- **PEOPLES PARK CARAVAN VILLAGE, CORAL BAY**

Go to Peoples Park Caravan Village in Coral Bay if you want to go somewhere out of season, but still want to soak in warm ocean waters without being stung.

It is located at the southern end of the magnificent Ningaloo Reef and has ideal weather all year long.

Don't miss Swimming with loggerhead turtles, reef sharks, manta rays, and whale sharks.

Lot 11, Robinson Street, Coral Bay, phone: (08) 9942 5933, from $32 per night.

Queensland

- ### <u>CAIRNS COCONUT HOLIDAY RESORT</u>

A parent's dream is this multi-award-winning BIG4 camping campground.

You rarely notice the kids there since there are so many things to keep them occupied.

Even though this resort is only seven minutes from the town center, you won't want to leave because there are so many free activities available, such as three swimming pools, tennis courts, an 18-hole minigolf course, volleyball, badminton, basketball, a huge adventure playground, an enormous jumping pillow, outdoor movies, and others.

Don't miss A tour around the 28 acres of meticulous landscapes, tropical gardens, and rainforest habitats.

Corner of Bruce Highway and Anderson Road, Cairns, (07) 4054 6644, from $36 per night.

- ### <u>DALRYMPLE TOURIST VAN PARK, CHARTERS TOWERS</u>

You're in for country hospitality and first-rate (clean) facilities at the Park, which is less than two kilometers from Charters

Towers' old mining district. This is the Park's award-winning point of distinction.

The proprietors, Gayle and Don Peters, really go beyond to make visitors feel at home. They offer excellent service, whether it is by giving information about the local landmarks or by putting just selected flowers in the restrooms for the women.

Toasting marshmallows over Dalrymple's campfire is a must-do activity because it's a terrific place to meet other travelers.

24 Dalrymple Road, Charters Towers, (07) 4787 1121, from $25 per night.

- ## **1770 CAMPING GROUND**

Happy campers pass each other at the shower block in this tiny gem and shout, "Another day in paradise!"

It more than makes up for in natural features, allowing campers to unwind and ponder. Visitors can catch their own mud crabs and fish for dinner.

To reserve a site directly on the beach, though, call as soon as possible because these sell out rapidly.

A day excursion to Lady Musgrave Island is a must-do.

Details: *641 Captain Cook Drive, Agnes Water, (07) 4974 9286, from $27 per night.*

- ## NOOSA TEWANTIN CARAVAN PARK

Noosa was founded as a commune for hippies in the 1960s; however, unlike Byron Bay, the hippies have completely been replaced by yuppies now.

Noosa's relaxed atmosphere hasn't changed, but its costs have skyrocketed. This Park offers visitors a low-cost lodging option only a short distance from the town's center.

A visit to the Eumundi Markets and a stroll down Hastings Street amid the stunning people are not to be missed.

Information: *(07) 5449 8060, 143 Moorindil Street, Tewantin, starting at $28 per night.*

Northern Territory

- ## KAKADU LODGE AND CARAVAN PARK

Kakadu's natural splendor is unmatched as a wilderness destination, regardless of whether you visit during the wet or dry season.

Why not stay in the middle of this World Heritage Site when exploring it? Kakadu Lodge, which is situated on the edge of

Jabiru Township and three hours west of Darwin, is the ideal location for reaching the entire Park.

After a day of sightseeing, you may unwind in the Park at the Poolside Bar and Bistro, which is surrounded by lush tropical plants, or by the lagoon-style pool (no Crocs here!).

Tour Ubirr to see some of Kakadu's breathtaking rock art galleries.

Information: *Jabiru Drive, Kakadu, (08) 8979 2422, from $32 per night.*

• **BATCHELOR RESORT, RUM JUNGLE**

Litchfield National Park is the destination for admirers of the outdoors who don't want to hike for hours on end in pursuit of the best waterfall or rock formation.

One of the oldest landscapes in the world, Batchelor Resort is the ideal starting point for exploring it.

In addition to having a mini-mart and fuel pump on-site (dispensing both unleaded and diesel fuel), this Park, which is only 15 minutes from Litchfield, makes it simple to travel by caravan. The Park can arrange for tour companies to pick up visitors from the Park's front entrance and return them at the end of the day.

Don't miss Florence Falls, the termite mounds, and the Lost City rock formations.

Details: *Rum Jungle Rd, Batchelor, (08) 8976 0123, from $30 per night.*

- ## **KNOTTS CROSSING RESORT, KATHERINE**

Katherine and its surroundings are a must-see for any traveler, known for its gushing waterfalls, towering red cliffs, and quirky boabs. At the center of it all, nestled within acres of tropical gardens and only a two-minute walk from the Katherine River, is Knotts Crossing Resort.

The Katherine River canoe trip, the Katherine Gorge cruise, the exploration of the Cutta Cutta caverns, or a soak in the neighboring hot springs are all activities you shouldn't miss.

Details: Corner of Giles and Cameron St., Katherine. From $30/night. (08) 8972 2511.

Victoria

- ### BEST FRIEND HOLIDAY RETREAT, YARRAM

Introducing Australia's first vacation spot created just for guests traveling with their furry companions! The Park features luxurious day-use kennels, enclosed off-leash training areas for dogs, a hydro-bath house, and a playground that is dog-friendly.

But because each caravan site is independently walled, you may leave your dog behind when you wish to explore some of the area's delights. To keep you and your dog entertained throughout your visit, the park managers regularly host a variety of dog contests.

Don't forget a visit to the neighborhood waterfall and a dip in the outdoor pool made of naturally occurring rocks.

Information: *Tarra Valley Rd, Tarra Valley, Yarram, Victoria, (03) 5186 1216, from $35 per night.*

- ### ANGLESEA BEACHFRONT FAMILY CARAVAN PARK

The Great Ocean Road is a byword for relaxing road trips. Travelers are enthralled by the views of southwest Victoria's eroding coastline and the old communities they pass. The

Anglesea Beachfront Family Caravan Park, which is tucked away among bushland and faces both the beach and the river, is located directly on this ancient road.

There are nearby mountain bike trails, bush treks, and Bells Beach, which is well known.

Anglesea Golf Course is a great place to play a round of golf, where you can pat kangaroos and look out at the ocean in between strokes.

Information: *(03) 5263 1583, 35 Cameron Rd, Anglesea, starting at $32 per night.*

- ## PHILLIP ISLAND CARAVAN PARK

It's no surprise Phillip Island has been rated one of Australia's best tourist attractions as it is home to the well-known Penguin Parade, Koala Conservation Center, Churchill Island historical farm, and Nobbies Center.

With its prime beachside location, an abundance of wildlife (including penguins, seals, koalas, and mutton birds), spotless amenities, and shaded campsites, the BIG4 camper park's staff makes it simple for visitors to take pleasure in their stay.

Don't miss The Penguin Parade. Every evening at dusk, the Little Penguins, the tiniest penguins in the world, arrive on land after a day of fishing at sea.

Information: *24 Old Bridge Rd, Newhaven, (03) 59567227, from $28 per night.*

South Australia

- ## ARKAROOLA TOURIST RESORT, FLINDERS RANGES

The Flinders Ranges, a group of rough mountains rising over green plains, date back more than 600 million years.

For more than 40.000 years, Aboriginal Dreamtime tales that describe how this region came to be have been passed down. Arkaroola Tourist Resort in the Northern Flinders Ranges has many eco-tourism-accredited guided excursions and some of Australia's most breathtaking mountain views.

As a natural refuge, this Park offers a wide range of activities (they even have three fully equipped observatories), whether you enjoy bird watching, bushwalking, geology, wildlife spotting, or 4WD excursions.

A five-course meal served outside near Wywhyana Creek and Wilpena Pound is Banquet in the Bush, which you shouldn't miss.

Information: *Northern Flinders Ranges, (08) 8648 4848, from $20 per night.*

- **TANUNDA CARAVAN AND TOURIST PARK, BAROSSA VALLEY**

Penfolds, Seppelt, Jacobs Creek, and Wolf Blass, to mention a few, are some of the best wines in the world and are produced in the Barossa.

This Park is tucked away less than an hour from Adelaide and only a short distance from charming Tanunda in the Barossa Valley. Visitors can rent bikes to explore the area's distinctive vineyard-covered slopes, rustic structures, Lutheran churches, and opulent wineries.

Therefore, remember to bring wine glasses on your upcoming caravanning trip.

Don't miss A Saturday morning visit to the farmers' market at the Vintners Sheds near Angaston, followed by a free glass of wine at one of the numerous cellar doors.

Info: *Barossa Valley Way, Tanunda, (08) 8563 2784, from $26 per night.*

- ## **ROBE LONG BEACH CARAVAN PARK**

The secluded beaches and fishing-village vibe of Robe have long drawn in savvy travelers.

Additionally, the Robe Long Beach Caravan Park runs at a slower pace than the township itself, allowing you to truly unwind. Being a BIG4 Holiday Park, the amenities are undoubtedly spotless and up to date, and the staff offers excellent customer service.

Just over 100 kilometers separate you from the Coonawarra Wine Region, Mount Gambier, and the Naracoorte Caves, but if you prefer to stay close to home, ancient Robe has a variety of quaint shops and restaurants. The BIG4 Caravan Parks provide fantastic regular bargains and specials, so be sure to visit their website (www.big4.com.au) frequently if you're interested in staying there.

Don't forget to go four-wheeling on the beaches and dune areas that border Little Dip, Conservation Park.

Information: *The Esplanade, Robe, from $29 per night, big4.com.au, (08) 8768 2237.*

Tasmania

- **DISCOVERY HOLIDAY PARK CRADLE MOUNTAIN**

This caravan park, which is the only one of its kind on Cradle Mountain, is well placed on the edge of the World Heritage-listed area, allowing visitors to easily explore the untamed nature.

You can even reserve horseback riding excursions at the front desk and Rent Mountain and quad bikes.

Enjoy the untamed wilderness with the possums and kangaroos who will greet you at your trailer door one evening while breathing some of the cleanest air in the entire globe.

The mesmerizing celestial show that fills the night sky is something you shouldn't miss.

Details: *Cradle Mountain Rd, (03) 6492 1395, from $35 per night.*

- ## WHITE BEACH TOURIST PARK, NUBEENA SOUTH

Port Arthur Historic Site, which was created by convicts, serves as a significant symbol of Australia's past.

It is one of Australia's top tourist destinations thanks to its restored structures and jail amenities. The park is only ten minutes from Port Arthur and is surrounded by white ghost gums, sandstone cliffs, and the open ocean, Still, after a long day of sightseeing, you just want to relax.

It's the ideal spot to lay your head down.

A terrifying ghost tour of Port Arthur is a must-do.

Details: *White Beach Rd, Nubeena South, (03) 6250 2142, from $26 per night.*

- ## STANLEY CABIN AND TOURIST PARK

Few people can claim to have slept beneath the ruins of a massive volcanic plug.

By pulling into Stanley Cabin and Tourist Park, directly below the amazing sight known as "The Nut," you may join this exclusive club.

This park is a birdwatcher's paradise since The Nut is a haven for migrating birds like shearwaters, kestrels, falcons, orange-bellied parrots, and fairy penguins. It is owned and run by helpful residents Fiona and Tim, who encourage visitors to explore the region.

Don't forget: Views of the entire coast can be had by ascending The Nut's 152m via the walkway (or chairlift).

Details: *Wharf Rd, Stanley, (03) 6458 1266, from $24 per night.*

- ## ST HELENS CARAVAN PARK

The Bay of Fires is comparable to a closely held secret that you are eager to share with everyone.

With its white sand beaches, glistening emerald waters, and red-capped rocks, it is the epitome of coastal perfection— without the throngs that are typically present in such locations. The award-winning St Helens Caravan Park is only ten minutes away.

This park has everything, whether it's fishing, swimming, or walking, that you're interested in. Hurry, though; the secret won't last long.

Lunch at Angasi Restaurant, which offers stunning views of the Bay of Fires, is a must-do.

Penelope St., St. Helens, (03) 6376 1290, from $27 per night.

Farmstays and Homestays

Australia has a wide variety of vacation experiences, from experiencing the Outback to unwinding on the Gold Coast beaches. Farmstays and homestays are two unusual vacation experiences that are becoming more and more popular in Australia.

Visitors have the chance to stay in a local home or on a working farm during farmstays and homestays, gaining firsthand knowledge of the culture and way of life there. In Australia, this kind of lodging is growing in popularity, especially with travelers who want to get away from the city's bustle and experience a slower pace of life.

Australian farmstays give guests the ability to interact closely with farm animals, take part in farm tasks like milking cows, gathering eggs, or shearing sheep, and discover sustainable farming methods. Through homestays, travelers can get a taste of the local cuisine, learn about local customs and culture, and interact with the neighborhood.

The chance to interact with locals and discover their way of life is one of the advantages of farmstays and homestays. A deeper awareness of the local way of life, customs, and history might improve tourists' overall vacation enjoyment.

Due to the fact that they frequently include meals and activities in the cost of the lodging, farmstays, and homestays can also be a more cost-effective choice for tourists. Families or people who are traveling on a budget may find this to be especially appealing.

Farmstays and homestays give tourists the ability to unplug from technology and the stresses of contemporary life in addition to the cultural and educational advantages. With options for hiking, horseback riding, and stargazing, this sort of lodging enables visitors to take their time and absorb the natural world around them.

In Australia, farmstays and homestays provide a distinctive and genuine tourism experience. A farmstay or homestay in Australia can be the ideal option for your next holiday if you're interested in sustainable agricultural methods, cultural immersion, or just the chance to unplug and refresh.

Visit www.tripadvisor.com to learn more about the Farmstays and Homestays listed below.

- ### **Gracefield Cottages**

**Category: Family Friendly Farm Stays & Self Catering Farm Stays**

Address: 135 Latrobe River Rd

Neerim South

Victoria

_3831_

Australia

A big farm with a variety of self-catering cottages is located right next to the Neerim State Forest, a fantastic spot for horseback riding and bush trekking, at Gracefield Farm Stay, which is only 30 minutes from Warragul, close to Melbourne, Victoria.

THE ACCOMMODATION:

They have a wonderful selection of tidy, cozy cottages that may accommodate up to 6 people. Every one of them includes a fully functional kitchen, bathroom, and living room with a flat-screen TV, DVD player, WiFi, and laundry facilities. There are patio areas and barbecue grills outside.

Although self-catering, they give the visitors a breakfast basket with eggs, bread, fresh fruit, jams & spreads, tea, and coffee to help them through the first morning.

There are herds of cattle and deer, as well as a wide variety of native species, spread across the farm's entire 97 acres of gorgeous green pastureland. Your hosts will be warm and hospitable, and they like showing visitors about the farm.

THE LOCATION:

Gracefield Farm Stay is a fantastic starting point for seeing some of Victoria's most picturesque rural places, in addition to the quiet joy of strolling around the farm and the surrounding woodlands.

The breathtaking Baw Baw National Park, to the east, features a sub-alpine plateau where you can enjoy skiing in the winter and bushwalking in the summer. Along with rock climbing, there are other locations where you may go horseback riding, canoeing, rafting, fishing, and more.

The Thompson River offers some of Victoria's best white water rafting and mushroom rock.

The Yarra Ranges, to the north, is home to cold temperate rainforests and the well-known mountain ash trees. Visit the Rainforest Gallery, which features a magnificent promenade where you may stroll by treetops and encounter a variety of species. On Lake Mountain in the Yarra, there are winter activities as well as some stunning waterfalls, especially at Keppel and Phantom Falls.

To the west is the equally fascinating Bunyip Park, and close to the farm stay are a number of lesser attractions, such as trout fishing at the Noojee trout farm, the Tooronga waterfalls, or the adorable village of Yarragon, which has some lovely cafes, bakeries, and stores.

The West Gippsland wine region, to the south, has more than a hundred vineyards and wineries, many of which provide tours and wine-tasting events. You can also find some of Victoria's best cuisine in this region.

From Melbourne's city center, it takes around an hour and a half to get to Gracefield Farm Stay.

- ## **RDC Vineyard Estate**

Category: B&B Farm Stays, Self-Catering Farm Stays, $ Vineyard Hotels

Address: 479 Hermitage Road
Pokolbin
New South Wales
2320
Australia

On its 25-acre vineyard estate and active winery, The Red Door Collective in Pokolbin offers upscale, boutique lodging for adults only (over 15s) with stunning views of the Brokenback Mountains.

There is an on-site cafe-diner serving modern Australian fusion food,' including filling all-day breakfasts and delicious fresh coffee, as well as a cellar door selling its own award-winning wines and offering casual, easygoing wine-tasting sessions.

THE ACCOMMODATION:

There are two private double suites (which can be combined if necessary) and two private 2-bedroom cottages (each of which can accommodate up to six people). All of them are exceptionally cozy, spotless, and well-appointed, and the cottages even have kitchens.

Although the cottage accommodations are self-catering, breakfast is offered as part of the fee for stays longer than two nights and offers both cooked and continental options.

All day long, the RDC cafe offers delicious, fresh food and coffee, and you may order picnic baskets to be delivered. Additionally, be sure to taste some of their well-regarded wines at the cellar door.

You can get a massage at the RDC in the seclusion of your own lodging or outside in the gardens. You can also rent one of their guest bicycles to explore the neighborhood of Pokolbin or join one of their guided cycling tours.

- ## **Daysy Hill Country Cottages**

Category: Family Friendly Farm Stays & Self Catering Farm Stays

Address: 2585 Cobden-Port Campbell Rd
Port Campbell
Victoria
3269
Australia

On its working farm near Port Campbell, Victoria, and close to the breathtaking scenery of the Great Ocean Road, Daysy Hill features a variety of very lovely, rustic-style self-catering cottages and apartments.

THE ACCOMMODATION:
The lodging options include roomy cottages that accommodate up to seven people and one-bedroom suites with spa baths. Visit the booking page to view them all in detail.

147

You'll discover that each one is spotless, cozy, fully furnished, and well-equipped. Most feature a small amount of outside space, and a few also enjoy excellent views of the nearby fields. WiFi, TV, cozy gas log fires, fully functional kitchens, and barbecues, as well as a sizable outside covered barbecue/kitchen area, are all provided as amenities.

THE LOCATION:

The farm is located less than two minute's drive from Port Campbell National Park, home to the renowned Twelve Apostles part of the Great Ocean Road, and the little town of Port Campbell. Less than 2.5 hours should be needed to travel from Melbourne.

- ## <u>Corynnia Station Farm Stay</u>

Category: B&B Farm Stays, Pet-Friendly Farm Stays, Family Friendly Farm Stays, and Self Catering Farm Stays
Address: 1823 Carrathool Rd
Carrathool
New South Wales
2711
Australia

This pet-friendly farm stay in New South Wales, Australia, on the border of the outback and midway between Sydney and Adelaide, is a terrific chance to see how a real Australian sheep station and sizable farm-producing irrigated crops operate.

THE ACCOMMODATION:

Modern conveniences, including five-star beds, heating, and cooling, may be found in every cottage. There are complete cooking and dining areas for self-catering, as well as meal hampers. The rates for the one and two-bedroom cottages include complimentary full breakfast buffets.

THE FARM:

Corynnia Station is a historic working station, and you can frequently have a tour of the farm with your hosts. A stunning garden oasis with a pool and tennis courts is also present. Pushbikes, amiable animals, bushwalking, breathtaking 360-degree vistas ideal for stargazing, as well as paddock picnics and campfires during the cooler months,

THE LOCATION:

The Corynnia Station Airstrip is where visitors can arrive by car—no 44 vehicle is necessary—or by direct private flight. There is no fuel supply within 65 kilometers of Corynnia Station; therefore, visitors must bring a full tank. Use GPS sparingly because it will not provide accurate journey times and instructions. Griffith and Hay may both be reached by car within 45 minutes from Corynnia Farm Station. Directions, in full detail, will be sent following the reservation.

- ## <u>Starline Alpacas Farm Stay Resort</u>

Category: Family Friendly Farm Stays, Self-Catering Farm Stays, and Farm Hotels with Spa,

Address: 1100 Milbrodale Rd

Broke

New South Wales

2330

Australia

This farm stay is a functioning alpaca farm with a few extra pleasures for visitors: a tennis court, sauna, jacuzzi, swimming pool, grill, and children's playground. It is located among the wineries of the Hunter Valley, New South Wales, Australia.

There are cottages available for lodging, each of which has a flat-screen TV in the living room, a full kitchen, and a balcony with outdoor seating. The animals are always happy to greet and be fed by visitors. The cottages have a view of the alpaca fields and are close by. At any moment during the day, visitors are welcome to interact with and feed the animals.

The welcome room, which also houses a gift shop and sells a variety of alpaca knitwear, has free WiFi.

- ## **The Heavens Mountain Escape**

Category: Family Friendly Farm Stays, Luxury Farm Stays, Farm Hotels with Spa, Pet-Friendly Farm Stays, Self-Catering Farm Stays, and Organic Farm Stays,

Address: 94 Paddington Lane
Kangaroo Valley
New South Wales
2577
Australia

On its own 160-acre, gloriously tranquil piece of Kangaroo Valley countryside, The Heavens provides opulent cottages with jacuzzi bathrooms. It is very much a place to unwind and rest, and while it can be a seductive romantic vacation from Sydney, it also gladly accommodates families.

THE ACCOMMODATION:

Two of the cottages have one bedroom, and one has two bedrooms. Each is roomy and completely self-contained, with top-of-the-line cooking amenities, a living area with satellite TV, plush beds, and spa baths or jacuzzis in the bathrooms.

Each one offers plenty of seclusion and privacy, as well as magnificent views of the surrounding farmland from the verandah outside and private BBQ facilities.

The cottages have views of the farm, which is home to kangaroos, of course, as well as wallaroos, wombats, wallabies, echidnas, and a variety of other native animals. Alpacas, goats, pigs, hens, ducks, and guinea fowl are all present.

Visitors are welcome to take a tour through the farm, meet some of the animals, go trekking through the bush, or treat themselves to a massage package from one of their available licensed masseuses.

THE LOCATION:

The Heavens is only 6 km from Kangaroo Valley town, and the entire area has lots to offer outdoor enthusiasts, including horseback riding, hiking, mountain biking, canoeing, rock climbing, fishing, and more. The scenery is also renowned for being breathtakingly beautiful everywhere.

Kangaroo Valley has a lot to offer both wine and cuisine enthusiasts. There are many vineyards in the area that provide wine tours, as well as some charming tiny villages with a rich cuisine culture, farmer's markets, etc.

- ## **Rocky Mountains Lodge**

*Category: **Family Friendly Farm Stays, Self-Catering Farm Stays, and Horse Riding Stays,***

Address: 24 Hillcrest View Ln.

Kangaroo Valley

New South Wales

2577 Australia

This tranquil, welcoming farm stay in New South Wales, close to Sydney, looks out over the Kangaroo Valley and offers lodge-style lodging on a working horse and cattle farm with some very stunning views of the surrounding countryside.

Horseback riding is a popular activity at the farm stay; you can arrange lessons and some of Australia's most picturesque trail rides, such as into the nearby Morton National Park, through rainforests, or even all the way to the top of Mt. Moollootoo. Children can ride one of their ponies too.

THE ACCOMMODATION:

Old-fashioned timber lodges that can accommodate up to eight people each have two separate double bedrooms and four single bunk beds in the living room. The self-catering lodging is in the shape of these lodges. In addition, there are two bathrooms, an open-concept kitchen and living room with a fireplace, and a barbeque area right outside the front door.

The smaller micro lodge contains a bathroom, an open-concept living room and kitchen, and a mezzanine floor with a queen bed above. In order to accommodate a total of four guests, the sofa in the living room also converts into a double bed. Additionally, there is a BBQ space right outside the entrance.

There is no WiFi for a digital detox.

THE FARM:

There are many horses and a herd of cattle on the farm, which is in operation. The proprietors are horse experts and aficionados with years of riding, instructing, and riding around the neighborhood.

The property itself has areas of open pasture land, rainforest, and open wilderness that go into Morton National Park and continue on to Mt. Moollootoo.

The proprietors are delighted to show you around the numerous beautiful routes, which all combine to make it a really unique location for horseback riding. You may climb Mt. Moollootoo to its summit, where the views of Morton Park, the Kangaroo River, and Lake Yurunga are just breathtaking.

There are a few amiable farm dogs there as well, and kangaroos and other native wildlife can be seen in plenty there.

THE LOCATION:

The location for a farm stay rural getaway in New South Wales couldn't be finer; it's perched on the slopes of Mt. Moollootoo and overlooks the lovely green Kangaroo Valley.

For those who enjoy the great outdoors, the Kangaroo Valley has a lot to offer: horseback riding, of course, as well as hiking, mountain biking (you can rent bikes from the farmstay), canoeing, rock climbing, fishing, etc., and the scenery is absolutely stunning. There are numerous unique bird species to witness, as well as kangaroos, platypuses, wombats, and a variety of other wildlife.

Wine tours may be arranged for a number of the local vineyards, including the award-winning Yarrawa Estate, which is located approximately 20 minutes away. Additionally, there are several great small towns nearby with a vibrant culinary culture, farmer's markets, etc., as well as a golf course at Moss Vale that is only 15 minutes away. Ask the friendly farm stay proprietors for recommendations and advice.

The best of Kangaroo Valley, which is frequently referred to as Australia's most beautiful Valley and is a very special site for many, sits right outside Rocky Mountain Lodge. If you prefer the gorgeous coastal route, the M1, it will take you around two and a half hours to get to the farm stay from Sydney along the M31 and the B31. It takes the M23 just under 2.5 hours to get there from Canberra before getting on the B31 outside of Moss Vale.

- ## **Brigadoon Farm Retreat**

Category: Family Friendly Farm Stays & Self Catering Farm Stays

Address: 43 Andalusian Retreat

Brigadoon

Western Australia

6069

Australia

The edge of the renowned Swan Valley wine trail is where you'll find this tranquil, quiet farm stay close to Perth. In fact, it takes less time to get to the airport than it does to the center of Perth.

THE ACCOMMODATION:

The lodging is in the shape of an "executive suite," a roomy and opulent self-catering chalet with a private entrance, a big living area with a DVD player and a flat-screen satellite TV, a well-equipped kitchen, and a double bedroom and bathroom. There is WiFi available everywhere, even on the patio outside, which has a full-size hot tub that looks out over the gardens and a private dining area.

THE FARM:

It's a very quiet, tranquil, and leisurely place to get away from the city. There is lots of room for you to go around the farm, where you can see, among other things, alpacas, horses, and hens, as well as the gardens, which offer a BBQ area. Additionally, the farm offers bike rentals for those who want to explore the stunningly rural surroundings.

THE LOCATION:

The proprietors can provide you with helpful advice for things to do and see around. The region is known as the Swan Valley, one of Australia's best wine-producing regions.

Although the Brigadoon proprietors don't produce their own wine, they can nevertheless suggest some excellent Swan Valley wine and cuisine trips as well as some other nearby attractions.

There are several vineyards nearby, as well as attractions like the Bells Rapids path, which is only a 15-minute drive from the farmstay. The Caversham Wildlife Park is also only a 30-minute drive away. It should be noted that having a car is a good idea in this area because, although being close to the city, it is still fairly remote and there are few possibilities for public transportation.

- ## **Blackwattle Farm Stay**

Category: B&B Farm Stays, Pet-Friendly Farm Stays, Organic Farm Stays, Family Friendly Farm Stays, and Self Catering Farm Stays

Address: 123 Old Peachester Rd

Beerwah

Queensland

4519

Australia

This little (by Australian standards!) farm with cows, alpacas, pigs, and hens has a large, roomy apartment nearby Brisbane, Queensland, on Australia's Sunshine Coast, and is only 10 minutes from Steve Irwin's Australia Zoo.

THE ACCOMMODATION:

There are three options available. There is a stylish, contemporary, and roomy suite with a private lounge space that has a flat-screen TV, DVD player, and iPod dock. A kitchenette and en suite bathroom with a lovely claw foot bathtub are also included.

The cozy "tiny house on wheels" contains two bedrooms, one of it is with a queen bed then the other with two single beds. You'll discover a TV, reverse-cycle air conditioning, a full kitchenette, and a BBQ on the spacious patio outside. Last, but not least, it contains a tiny bathroom with a shower and a composting (odorless!) toilet.

The "tiny house on wheels" lodging has steps and a ladder; thus, children under the age of seven should not stay there.

The cottage, which includes two bedrooms with a king-sized bed in one and two king-sized single beds in the other, is the last option. Along with a kitchen and living area, it offers a lovely bathroom with a claw-foot bathtub. A sizable outdoor patio area with chairs and a grill is located outside.

Visitors get access to the entire farm and are welcome to assist with duties like collecting fresh eggs and feeding the animals. Additionally, they have a garden of organic vegetables, and the welcoming owners host workshops on how to grow your organic garden at home.

The farm has a communal room with reading and board games, and WiFi is available throughout. Although the lodging is self-catering, you will be given a fantastic organic breakfast every morning as part of the fee. On request, breakfast and BBQ supper hampers can also be provided.

THE LOCATION:

As previously noted, the farm is ideally located just 10 minutes from the renowned Australia Zoo, a must-see attraction in the region. The Glass House Mountains, the Blackall Range, and the charming communities of Montville and Maleny are all within easy driving distance and offer fantastic hiking opportunities and breathtaking views.

Given that this is the well-known Sunshine Coast, there are numerous excellent beaches close by that you can get to in less than 30 minutes.

- ## **Mount Bundy Station**

Category: Farm Glamping, Horse Riding Stays, Family Friendly Farm Stays, and Self Catering Farm Stays

Address: 315 Haynes Rd

Adelaide River

Northern Territory

0846

Australia

In Australia's far north, close to Darwin, Mount Bundy Station offers a welcoming, pleasurable farm stay experience along the banks of the Adelaide River. Due to its location between Darwin and the Kakadu and Litchfield National Parks, it attracts a sizable number of tourists who stay overnight at its sizable functioning cattle farm station and take farm tours.

THE ACCOMMODATION:

There are divers types of lodging options available for a group of up to eight people per unit, including rooms, self-catering cottages, and glamping tents. And they all have access to a sizable communal kitchen.

If you'd like, the helpful personnel at the tour desk may arrange for you to spend the day fishing or taking a horse-drawn tour of the farm. Additionally, you can get a quality breakfast package at reception if you don't feel like cooking in the morning.

There is no WiFi; please note!

THE LOCATION:

The farm serves as a convenient starting point for trips to the well-known Adelaide River region and Litchfield National Park. The park is around 20 miles away, and day trips by 4WD can be planned directly from the farm. Highlights include exploring the creeks on foot, taking a dip in Florence and Wangi Falls, and swimming in the area's numerous rock pools. Another enjoyable excursion is a 4WD tour of Butterfly Gorge's thermal baths, where you may swim and keep an eye out for the area's plethora of wildlife, particularly birds.

And there are a ton more locations to explore in this gorgeous natural setting. You can also arrange horseback riding excursions closer to home; for instance, you can travel to the adjacent Robin Falls via Dorat Rd and take in some of the lovely, serene scenery en route. The farm owners can arrange everything for you and are always available to offer advice and helpful recommendations.

- ## **Mt. Hay Retreat**

Category: Luxury Farm Stays, Farm Hotels with Spa, and Self Catering Farm Stays

Address: 260 Mount Hay Road, Broughton Vale

Berry

New South Wales

2535

Australia

The unique rural retreat in the heart of Kangaroo Valley is the adults-only, green Mt. Hay Retreat close to Berry Village. It provides extremely opulent self-catering lodging in great locations on its 360-acre private estate, which includes groomed gardens, farmland, woodlands, and some breathtaking views. A 33-meter heated indoor pool, spa services, and a massive chess board on the grounds are available amenities.

The Mt. Hay Retreat is only open to visitors who are at least 18 years old.

THE ACCOMMODATION:

As an adult-only resort, Mt. Hay places a strong focus on seclusion and meaningful alone time. They feature a total of 5 double rooms that are all individually contained and highly private, known as Deluxe King Suites.

As you can see from the pictures, they are all exquisitely constructed, roomy, and very well furnished with HD LCD TVs, WiFi, reverse cycle air conditioning, chic kitchenettes (with Nespresso coffee makers), private outdoor terraces with open-air baths, and some incredibly plush bathrooms with luxury toiletries and bathrobes, some of which include a spa bath.

The resort has a 30-meter heated pool as well as top-notch spa facilities where you may book a variety of health and cosmetic treatments.

The 360-acre estate, with its wonderfully maintained gardens, orchards, cattle farm, woodlands, and hidden glades and dams, can keep you occupied for many enjoyable hours.

You will undoubtedly see some of the local wildlife, such as wombats, kookaburras, wedge-tailed eagles, lyre birds, black cockatoos, echidnas, and even some rare brush-tailed rock wallabies, in addition to visiting the farm animals—cows, goats, and hens.

THE LOCATION:

Mt. Hay Retreat is in a prime location, in the shadow of Broughton Head, with views that extend to the South Coast's hills and the ocean beyond. This is especially true given that Berry Village, one of Kangaroo Valley's most charming communities, is only five minutes away by car.

Famous restaurants, cozy cafes, and some of the Valley's best boutique shopping are all available there. Additionally, there are numerous wineries in the area, with the Coolangatta Estate and Crooked River Winery serving as two of the best examples, and a variety of outdoor activities, like hot air ballooning and boat trips, are available. For all of the aforementioned things and more, your hosts at Mt. Hay can point you on the correct route.

The coast and several fantastic beaches are also close by; it takes less than an hour to get to Jervis Bay from Shoalhaven Heads and Seven Mile Beach.

Driving there from Sydney should take less than two hours.

Chapter 4: Sydney

Introduction to Sydney

With a metro population of roughly 4.28 million, Sydney is the most populated city in Australia. The state capital of New South Wales is Sydney. Sydney, the first European settlement in Australia, was founded in 1788 at Sydney Cove by Arthur Phillip, the captain of the British First Fleet.

On the southeast coast of Australia, Sydney is situated. The term "the Harbor City" comes from the fact that the city is constructed around Port Jackson, which encompasses Sydney Harbor. The Australian Stock Exchange is located there, making it Australia's biggest financial hub. The top industries in Sydney's economy include manufacturing, retail, tourism, real estate and business services, and health and community services.

Sydney is a popular worldwide travel destination known for its beaches and the Sydney Opera House and Harbor Bridge, which are twin landmarks. The metropolitan region has numerous bays, rivers, and inlets, and it is surrounded by national parks. According to the Loughborough University group's 1999 inventory, it has been designated as a global city. Numerous major international sporting events have taken place in the city, including the 1938 British Empire Games, the 2000 Summer Olympics, and the 2003 Rugby World Cup.

One of the world's places with the most different kinds of people, Sydney serves as a key entry point for immigrants to Australia. Sydney ranks as the twenty-first most expensive city in the world and as the most expensive city in Australia, according to the Mercer Cost of Living report. A Sydneysider is someone who lives in the city.

Geography

Sydney is located in a coastal basin that is surrounded by the Woronora Plateau to the south, the Hawkesbury River to the north, the Blue Mountains to the west, and the Pacific Ocean to the east. Sydney is located on a submerged shoreline where deep river valleys (rias) carved into the Hawkesbury sandstone have been flooded by the rising sea level. The biggest natural harbor in the world is Port Jackson, which is one of these submerged valleys and is also known as Sydney Harbor. In the urban region, there are more than 70 port and ocean beaches, including the well-known Bondi Beach. As of 2001, Sydney's urban area covered 651 mi2. The Central Coast and Blue Mountains are located in this region, along with large tracts of national parks and other undeveloped territory.

Geographically, Sydney is divided into two main areas: the Hornsby Plateau, a sandstone plateau mostly to the north of the harbor, and the Cumberland Plain, a comparatively flat region to the south and west of the harbor, divided by steep valleys. The North Shore was slower to develop due to its mountainous topography and was primarily a quiet backwater until the Sydney Harbor Bridge was built in 1932, connecting it to the rest of the city. The oldest parts of the city are situated in the flat plains south of the harbor.

Climate

Sydney experiences a humid subtropical climate with warm summers, moderate winters, and yearly rainfall. More extreme temperatures are recorded in the inland western suburbs, where the weather is less softened by proximity to the ocean. The hottest month is January, with an average air temperature range of 18.6 °C to 25.8 °C at Observatory Hill and an average of 14.6 days each year with temperatures above 30 °C. When a four-day countrywide heat wave came to an end on January 14, 1939, the highest temperature ever recorded was 45.3 °C. Temperatures rarely fall below 5 °C in coastal locations during the relatively cool winter. July is the coolest month, with an average temperature range of 8.0 °C-16.2 °C. The recorded minimum temperature was 2.1 °C. The amount of rainfall varies throughout the seasons pretty evenly, with the first half of the year seeing a modest increase due to the predominance of easterly winds. With moderate to low fluctuation, the average annual rainfall is 1217.0 millimeters (47.9 in), falling on a yearly average of 138.0 days.

Urban structure

For addressing and postal purposes, Sydney's vast area is technically divided into more than 300 suburbs, which are further divided into 38 local government regions for administration. There is no single city administration, although the Government of New South Wales and its agencies are heavily involved in providing services to the metropolitan area. The CBD and surrounding inner-city suburbs make up the relatively modest area that the City of Sydney itself occupies. Additionally, informal regional designations are employed to conveniently characterize bigger urban areas. The Eastern Suburbs, the Hills District, the Inner West, the Lower North Shore, the Northern Beaches, the North Shore, St. George, the South of Sydney, the South of Eastern Sydney, the South of Western Sydney, Sutherland Shire, and Western Sydney are among these. However, none of these categories readily include a lot of suburbs.

From Sydney Cove, the location of the first European settlement, the CBD of Sydney extends southward for roughly 1.25 miles. Several parks, notably Wynyard and Hyde Park, are dotted among the densely packed skyscrapers and other buildings, including iconic historic sandstone structures like the Sydney Town Hall and Queen Victoria Building. A chain of parkland that runs from Hyde Park through the Domain and Royal Botanic Gardens to Farm Cove on the harbor encircles Sydney's central business district on its east side. Darling Harbour, a well-known tourist destination and entertainment district, borders the west side of the CBD, while Central Station delineates its southern boundary. Sydney's central business district's principal north-south artery is George Street. Although the CBD predominated the city's commercial and cultural activity in its early years, following World War II, additional commercial and cultural areas have grown radially. As a result, from more than 60% at the conclusion of World War II to less than 30% in 2004, fewer white-collar occupations were concentrated in the CBD. The most important outer business districts are Parramatta in the central west, Blacktown in the west, Bondi Junction in the east, Liverpool in the southwest, Chatswood to the north, and Hurstville to the south. North Sydney's commercial district is also connected to the CBD by the Harbor Bridge.

Iconic Landmarks and Attractions

- ## The Sydney Opera House

It's one of the best sites to visit in Sydney and the top option among Sydney landmarks. When Sydney is mentioned, most people immediately picture the Sydney Opera House. It is also among the most well-known structures in the entire world. It is a UNESCO World Heritage Site and one of Sydney's top tourist destinations. Depending on your imagination, the building may depict several images. When asked about the geometry of this structure, there were no incorrect responses. Some people think it's a sea shell, while others envision wind-swept sails.

- ## The Rocks

The Australian "the rocks" differs from the American "the rock." It's a stunning historic region with lovely architecture rather than a well-known wrestler and actor. Visit this location on the weekend to take advantage of The Rocks Market's shopping opportunities. There is the Justice and Police Museum if you enjoy culture and history. You can view Australia's criminal history at this museum. Visit Pancakes on The Rocks for a great and substantial brunch. Pubs are another notable feature of this neighborhood. The Fortune of War and Lord Nelson are two of Sydney's allegedly oldest bars.

- ## Sydney Tower Eye

The Sydney Tower Eye, formerly known as the Centrepoint Tower, is a fantastic location to view Sydney from a great height. It offers both a panoramic perspective and a magnificent 360-degree panorama of Sydney. At the top of the tower, binoculars allow you to see the city more clearly. The "4-D" presentation, which mimics a fly around the city, is also included in the price of entrance to the tower. Fun fact: It wasn't until 2011 that the term "eye" was added to the name of the organization.

- **Queen Victoria Building**

One of Sydney's most famous structures is the Queen Victoria Building. In fact, it would be difficult to find a structure that is more recognizable than this one. It was constructed in the 1890s as a cathedral-sized municipal market. The structure now provides a luxurious, high-end shopping experience. The structure itself is a famous piece of architecture. There are numerous features that give this structure a distinctive vibe. It's always a good idea to stop by this building, even if you don't want to shop. A visitor is never unimpressed with this structure.

- **Sydney Harbour Bridge**

Before the Sydney Opera House was constructed, the Sydney Harbour Bridge was Sydney's most well-known landmark and was frequently referred to as the Coathanger. Its building process began in 1923 and was completed in 1932. It is currently among the largest steel arch bridges. You can wander in quiet because the bridge's two ends have large double peers. You can reserve a bridge climb if you're looking for a beautiful and magnificent view. Can lift passengers to the 135-meter-high arch's summit. Do not forget to include this location on your list of Sydney landmarks.

- **Sydney Observatory**

In the heart of Sydney, a hill known as Observatory Hill is where Sydney Observatory is situated. It transforms into an astronomical observatory from a fort that was constructed on "Windmill Hill" in the early 19th century. It now serves as an operating museum where visitors can view the stars and planets at night. The Observatory houses two telescopes: a cutting-edge 40 cm Schmidt-Cassegrain and a vintage 29 cm refractor constructed in 1874. In fact, it is Australia's oldest telescope still in continuous service. The observatory tours typically begin at night and last for 90 minutes. The trips include a planetarium visit, a look via a telescope, and a dome tour.

- **Powerhouse Museum**

The Central Business District of Sydney is where the museum is situated. Without a doubt, this is a fantastic and intriguing museum to visit when in Sydney. "Museum of Applied Arts & Sciences" is what it is called. Its collection of exhibits is enormous. Decorative arts, science, communication, transportation, costumes, furniture, media, computer

179

technology, and space technology are all represented in the collection. If you want to find out more about the history, culture, and way of life of Australia, come here. Even if you're not interested in history and culture, going to this museum is a lot of fun.

- **The Blue Mountains**

This gorgeous location is only 50 kilometers west of Sydney. Australia received the Blue Mountains as a gift from nature. This is the place to go if you're seeking a breathtaking view and some outdoor adventure. It can be an excellent place to retreat from Sydney's summer heat. There is a lengthy list of locations you must see while here. Wentworth Falls, the Three Sisters, the incline railway, cafes, a bakery, and a sweets shop in Leura, as well as the Everglades, are examples of such locations. A lover of the outdoors? Take a journey to the Blue Mountains and immerse yourself in the breathtaking environment while you're there.

The top Blue Mountains tour to fully experience Sydney's natural beauty

There are many things you need to get ready before the trip! You'll definitely find our post on "things you need to know about the Blue Mountains" useful.

- **The National Maritime Museum**

Anyone looking to tour in Sydney will find a fantastic experience at the National Maritime Museum. This museum

181

can be found near Sydney Harbor, together with many other well-known tourist destinations. The museum is packed with fascinating exhibits and features that will undoubtedly make you have a great time. The museum exhibits the marine history of Australia, particularly specifically Sydney, as its name would imply. It demonstrates how Australia's maritime sector has grown from the first settlers' arrival through the growth of the Australian Navy. The staff is also incredibly kind, passionate, and knowledgeable. And the best part is that admission is really inexpensive. Consequently, you can enjoy a wonderful experience at a fair price.

- **Hyde Park**

Hyde Park, which was named after London's Hyde Park, is located in the center of the bustling CBD. Perhaps Australia's oldest park is this one. The ANZAC Memorial building and visitor center, together with a number of other monuments and statues, are all located in the southern part of Hyde Park. The landmark Archibald Fountain and several theme gardens featuring public artworks, monuments, and water features may be found in the northern part of the park. There are about 580 mature native and exotic trees there. The park also hosts a number of cultural occasions throughout the year, such as Australia Day and the Sydney Festival. It is undoubtedly a well-known destination; visitors come from all over the world to take in the diverse sights and sounds.

- **New South Wales Art Gallery**

The Sydney Art Gallery of New South Wales is located to the east of Hyde Park. It is a treasure trove of different kinds of art in both permanent and passing visitor collections. Numerous art collections, particularly colonial-era Australian art, are housed there. The Yiribana Gallery also houses a sizable collection of Aboriginal artwork along with Asian and European works of art. Although there is no entrance price, some transient exhibits could charge a modest fee. Daily hours at the Art Gallery are typically 9 am to 5 pm. Therefore, plan your schedule accordingly because you do not want to miss this location when traveling.

• St. Mary's Cathedral

The St. Mary's Cathedral is located facing Hyde Park. This location serves as a reminder of the Catholic Church's humble beginnings in Australia. The location serves as the Sydney Archbishop's residence as well. The building style is representative of the 19th-century Gothic Revival. A perforated parapet finishes the higher roofline. The structure was based on Lincoln Cathedral and included twin spires on one of its ends. The choice to glaze the clerestory with yellow glass was made at the outset due to the intensity of Australian sunlight. Its facade bears a resemblance to the Notre Dame Cathedral in Paris. It becomes a landmark from all angles.

• Kings Cross

King Cross, sometimes known as "The Cross" by locals, is located about two kilometers east of Sydney's CBS. This location is Sydney's diverse and historically significant red light district. It was an artistic neighborhood until the 1950s, when Beatniks made it a hotspot. It has a reputation for being less than appetizing at night, but during the day, it presents a different image. Diners from nearby hostels congregate at cafes, motels, and chic eateries. Simply locate the large Coca-Cola billboard at William Street and Darlinghurst Road to get here. The "Gateway to The Cross" is how the locals refer to it.

- **Museum of Contemporary Art Australia**

A museum in Australia completely devoted to displaying, understanding, and collecting contemporary art is called the Museum of Contemporary Art Australia. Its exhibits come from all over the world and Australia. On the western edge of Circular Quay, it is located in the old Maritime Services Board Building, an art deco structure. The museum received a A$58 million expansion and redevelopment beginning in 2010 after it first opened. Since 1989, it has acquired nearly 4,000 pieces by Australian artists for its collection. Paintings, photos, sculptures, works on paper, and moving pictures are all included in the collection. Works by Aboriginal and also Torres Strait Islander artists are also included.

- **SEA LIFE Sydney Aquarium**

The SEA LIFE Aquarium is another must-see location in Sydney. Sydney Aquarium is a fantastic place to see aquatic life. It has five exhibits, each representing a distinct habitat, such as an ocean, estuary, or river. It's also among the best places to take children. You can enjoy the various marine life while having an underwater experience here. Numerous types of mammals, fish, and other animals can be found there. Make sure you don't miss it because you may observe the aquatic animals being fed here. The aquarium is also easily accessible because of its proximity to Circular Quay.

- **Government House Sydney**

The Government House Sydney is a short distance from the lovely botanic garden. One of Australia's best-preserved and well-maintained colonial-style buildings is this one. Its construction began in 1846, and 27 governors have lived there since then. Sydney's "hidden jewel" is this stunning structure with its internal Gothic influences. With tall trees and brilliant colors, the building's surrounding garden is likewise quite beautiful. High-profile international visitors are hosted in this building, where important government meetings also take place. There are very few excursions available to see the inside of the structure. Therefore, think about making early bookings to ensure that you get a position on this excursion.

- **Darling Harbour**

The majority of Sydney's must-see locations may be found at Darling Harbour, a pedestrianized area. The Chinese Garden of Friendship, the Australian National Maritime Museum, and even the Wild Life Sydney Zoo are located nearby. Additional interesting attractions include an IMAX and 9D theater, waterfront jet boat rides, virtual flights, and racing vehicle adventures. You can stroll down the pier and enjoy the wind if you don't feel like going somewhere. It will be pleasant and energizing to breathe in the salty sea air.

- ## The Royal Botanic Garden Sydney

There isn't much else close to the city that gives natural floral splendor save Central Park. The garden is a short distance from the CBD (Central Business District). In the middle of a hectic metropolis, it's one of the ideal spots to just relax and take in nature. The garden is evidently alive with life. Birds abound in the woods, and you can spot foxes perched on their limbs. There are also specialty gardens, each of which focuses on a certain aspect of the plant kingdom. Begonias, palms, roses, and ferns are among the plants on display. You should absolutely pay this site a visit because of how amazing the garden feels.

• ANZAC War Memorial

The primary commemorative military structure in Australia is the ANZAC War Memorial. It is located near the southernmost point of Hyde Park. Massive sculptures and figural reliefs by Rayner Hoff adorn its facade. As a tribute to the Australian Imperial Force during World War I, it was constructed. If you're visiting Sydney to learn more about its past, you must see this building.

• Barangaroo Reserve

At the northernmost point of Barangaroo is the 6-hectare reconstructed headland park known as Barangaroo Reserve. It's a wonderful place for a stroll with a stunning perspective and a terrific illustration of an urban renewal project done well. It was given that name in honor of a powerful indigenous woman leader during the era of European colonization. The Wulugul Walk is one of the most well-liked activities here. It's a foreshore promenade that, once finished, would give pedestrians unrestricted access to a lovely 14-kilometer walk along the harbor from Garden Island to the Fish Markets.

- ## Sydney Town Hall

Sydney, the state capital of New South Wales, is home to the Sydney Town Hall, a 19th-century structure. In addition to council offices and conference spaces, it also houses the Sydney Lord Mayor's chambers. This structure is located on George Street, across from the Queen Victoria Building, in Sydney's financial center. There are many retail stores and entertainment venues nearby. The Town Hall's steps are a well-liked gathering spot. Even now, Sydney's city center still uses it as a key gathering spot.

- ## Great Synagogue

Sydney's The Great Synagogue is a sizable synagogue. It starts from Elizabeth Street and reaches Castlereagh Street on the other side of Hyde Park. This structure was created by Cornish architect Thomas Rowe, and it was dedicated in 1878. Byzantine and Gothic features are combined in the synagogue's architecture.

- ## Luna Park

The biggest draw in this area may be seen without entering the park. What you're here to see and adore is the gate. The park's entry gate has a slightly eerie vibe to it. It is one of just two theme parks in the world that is covered by legal protection. You are still welcome to enter the park if the gate intrigues you. Numerous structures in this area are included on the NSW State Heritage Register and the Register of the National Estate. The park is frequently used to film television and motion picture projects.

• Macquarie Street

The most fashionable street in Sydney used to be this one. At each end of it are Hyde Park and the Sydney Opera House. Lachlan Macquarie, a former governor of New South Wales, is honored by the name Macquarie Street. Hyde Park Barracks and St. James' Church were two of the structures Macquarie ordered. At the southern end of Macquarie Street, the two structures are situated across Queen's Square from one another. A stroll down this street may be a wonderful experience if you're trying to get from Hyde Park to the opera theater.

• St. James Church

Sydney's inner-city St. James Church is an Anglican parish church. The parish church, which bears the name of St. James the Great, was established in 1835. This building was created by Francis Greenway, a convict who was transported in the manner of a Georgian town church. It is a part of the Macquarie Street historic district, which also contains other structures from the early colonial era. Its initial ministry was to Sydney's convict population, and over the years, it has remained committed to helping the city's needy and disadvantaged.

- **Parramatta**

Sydney's multicultural district of Parramatta has a burgeoning art and cinema industry. Numerous hip pubs, restaurants, and artsy cafes may be found here. Along the river are historic sites and walking and cycling lanes. Those who appreciate art and film should visit this location without a doubt.

- **George Street**

The oldest street in Australia, located in the CBD, is home to several historic buildings. The 3-kilometer-long roadway connects several of the most significant structures and areas of the city. George Street runs from Sydney's northernmost point to its southernmost point. You can see a lot of buildings in this area. But if you want to see a variety of architectural styles, be sure to check out the Town Hall, St Andrews Cathedral, and The Strand Arcade.

• Sydney Cenotaph

In Martin Place stands the Sydney Cenotaph. It's also one of Sydney's oldest memorials to World War I. It appears as a single stone block with a sepulchral shape. Two bronze statues of a soldier and a sailor standing at either end of the monument guard the cenotaph. Here, memorial ceremonies are frequently held. Most significantly, it serves as the focal point for Sydney's major ANZAC and Armistice Day dawn services, which bring tens of thousands of visitors.

• Mrs. Macquarie's Chair

It is an exposed sandstone rock that has been carved into the shape of a bench and is also known as Lady Macquarie's Chair. It is located in Sydney Harbour on a peninsula. In truth, Mrs. Macquarie's Point is the name of the peninsula. For Elizabeth Macquarie, the wife of Major-General Lachlan Macquarie, the governor of New South Wales, it was hand-carved by prisoners in 1810. A stone inscription mentioning Mrs. Macquarie's Road is located above the chair. It connected Mrs. Macquarie's

Point to the original Government House, which is now the Museum of Sydney. Its erection was ordered by Governor Macquarie for the benefit of his wife.

- **Fort Denison**

A portion of Sydney Harbour National Park includes Fort Denison. It was formerly a prison and a defense building. The Royal Botanic Gardens are located northeast of the island where it is situated. The location has capabilities for a time gun, navigational aids, and tide gauges. Both the military and penitentiary establishments were created by George Barney. Anyone searching for a lesson in military history should visit this location.

Outdoor Activities and Adventures

- **Ocean pools**

Australia doesn't truly have a lot of shark attacks on record, despite popular opinion. According to the International Shark Attack File, the U.S. actually outranks Australia every year, with 47 attacks in 2021 compared to 12 in Australia.

But you can put on your "bathers" (one of many Aussie terms for a swimsuit, my preferred term is "togs") and head to one of the city's approximately three dozen dramatic ocean pools, many of which are indentations carved into the rocky shore if you don't want to risk any marine threats while admiring Sydney's dramatic ocean scapes.

The Bronte Baths, which were carved out of sandstone rocks just south of the coastal town of the same name and first opened in 1887, are one of the oldest. Admission is free. Wylie's Baths at adjacent Coogee, which opened in 1907, has a natural rock bottom and expansive views of the ocean. The cost of admission is $5.50 AUD ($4 for adults).

The Bondi Icebergs Pool, which is 50 meters (164 feet) long and bears the name of the neighborhood swimming club, is possibly the most well-known (and Instagrammed) of them. It was created in 1929. People practice their butterfly and backstroke to the beat of the tides as spray from the surf spills over the edge of the pool (admission costs AU$8, or $6). It's a terrific place to launch into the next endeavor on my list as well.

- **Bondi to Coogee Coastal walk**

One of Sydney's most well-known and pleasurable coastal treks is from the well-known beach district of Bondi southward into the relaxed surfing communities of Bronte and Coogee, each of which has its own expansive, golden sand beach.

It takes about 90 minutes to walk the entire 3.7 miles from Bondi to Coogee. Along the way, you'll pass lovely coves like Clovelly and the clifftop Waverley Cemetery, which has a grassy slope with macabre Victorian and Edwardian gravestones scattered throughout, including one for the renowned Australian author and poet Henry Lawson.

You can end your journey by spending some time at Bondi or Coogee's beaches, depending on which way you go. As an alternative, you may stop by the old Coogee Pavilion, which has been turned into a popular dining and drinking destination with multiple venues, for a drink after your ramble.

- **BridgeClimb's Burrawa Indigenous Experience**

Just four years after its predecessor, in 1932, the Sydney Harbour Bridge, which was modeled after the Tyne Bridge in Newcastle, England, opened with an arch span that was nearly three times as long (about 1,654 feet).

Even today, the Sydney Harbour Bridge links the city's financial core to the suburbs on the northern side of the waterway. On one of BridgeClimb's guided tours, including the 3.5-hour "Ultimate" experience, which costs AU$348 per adult

($257) and AU$189 per child (about $139), visitors may learn all about the 400-foot-high arch's history while they climb it.

The relatively recent Burrawa Indigenous Experience is one of the more distinctive climbs, allowing climbers to learn about the history of the Aboriginal peoples who lived in the region where Sydney now stands before European explorers reached these shores. Participants in the three-hour activity hear from Indigenous storyteller Shona Davidson, who is from the Quandamooka and Nunukal of North Stradbroke Island, about the origins of place names in the city as well as about the lives of illustrious Indigenous elders like Bennelong and Patyegarang.

Every month's last Saturday at 9:15 am and 1:45 pm, with extra days in April and July the tour is offered. A $10 donation ($7.40) is included in the ticket price for the non-profit Tribal Warrior Foundation, which provides development and mentorship programs for Indigenous youth and families in Sydney. Tickets cost AU$288 ($212) for adults and AU$149 ($110) for children.

- ### The Rocks Aboriginal Dreaming tour

If you'd rather stay on solid ground, you may learn about Australia's Indigenous past and the people who once lived in and took care of the region that is now Sydney on a walking tour of The Rocks neighborhood with Dreamtime Southern X. The founder Margret Campbell or one of her guides, will carry out a customary welcoming ritual that acknowledges the Earth Mother and explains the significance of ochre to Indigenous traditions. The following 90 minutes are spent teaching visitors about the daily lives and cultural practices of the region's first humans, how their stories of creation are woven into the landscape, and how these components may still be seen in Sydney today. Every day at 10:30 am and 1:30 pm, tours leave for AU$59 ($43.50) for adults and AU$33 ($24) for children.

- ### Take the ferry to Manly

Spend the day lounging on the sandy beach or taking it easy under the shade of the arrow-straight Norfolk pines that line Manly's Marine Parade by taking the 20- to 30-minute ferry ride from Circular Quay to the town of Manly (On Sydney Ferries, fares for adults range from $5.70 to $6.90 each way).

The Opera House, Harbour Bridge, and other famous Sydney sites can all be seen from the outdoor seating area of the boat. As you travel northeast toward the mouth of the harbor, you can also observe the city's different coastal villages as they pass by. After spending the day at the beach, stop by Hugos Manly, located right on the waterfront, for an early beachside supper of fresh Sydney rock oysters, kingfish sashimi, and unique wood-fired pizzas, such as one with chili-marinated roasted prawns and bell pepper.

- **Taronga Zoo**

You can spend an afternoon at Australia's renowned Taronga Zoo getting to know the animal residents of the continent a little better if your trip doesn't include time in the bush viewing Australia's distinctive flora and fauna (For visitors 16 and older, entry is AU$44.10, or roughly $32.50; for youngsters ages 4 to 15, it costs AU$26.10, or roughly $19.25). The round-trip adult fare for the 12-minute boat travel from Circular Quay ranges from $4.50 to $5.60.

The zoo is not only home to nearly 5,000 creatures representing more than 350 species, including Australian natives like koalas, red and tree kangaroos, and adorable small greater bilbies, but it also has some of the best city vistas.

- **Sunrise kayak and coffee**

By signing up for a sunrise kayak tour with Sydney by Kayak, you may use your jet lag to your advantage while enjoying a flat white or long black (or any other coffee beverage of your choice, really) at a nearby cafe.

Weather permitting, paddlers cross beneath the Harbour Bridge on weekdays from November through January and on weekends all year long as they paddle along Blues Point and Lavender Bay's coastline. Tours cost between AU$125 and AU$145 (about $92 and $107) per person and last for around two hours.

10 Best Museums in Sydney

This list of Sydney's top museums features some of the city's most significant art galleries, exhibition halls, and historical sites. You may bring the whole family to these museums to learn more about Australian history via the study of art, science, artifacts, and architecture.

The largest metropolitan area in Australia, Sydney features everything from world-famous beaches to shopping centers. If you want to learn more about the world, you can visit a lot of cultural locations. These museums are fantastic for a day trip with the family or a rainy Sydney activity, and they are definitely worth seeing while you are there.

Note: *Some of these museums already discussed under **Iconic Landmarks and Attractions** in this same chapter, we just provided here additional information about them.*

1. Australian National Maritime Museum

Harbourside museum with ship replicas

Good for: • History • Families • Photo

In Sydney's Darling Harbour, the Australian National Maritime Museum is a well-liked tourist destination. Explore some amazing ship reproductions at one of the world's largest and most varied in-water fleet museums.

Six permanent galleries at the museum also cover the development and operations of the Royal Australian Navy. It frequently hosts temporary exhibits and has a 3D theater where educational documentaries are shown. While touring the museum, are you becoming peckish? Visit the nearby Ripples Maritime Museum, which serves Western food, including paninis and hamburgers.

Address: *2 Murray Street, Sydney, New South Wales, 2000, Australia*

Open every day between 9.30 and 6 pm.

Phone: +61 (0)2 9298 3777

2. Museum of Contemporary Art Australia

View contemporary artwork in a stunning Art Deco structure.

Excellent for: • History • Families

One of the top museums for modern art in the nation is the Museum of Contemporary Art Australia. The former Maritime Services building now houses the museum, which is a late Art Deco structure and is situated at Circular Quay. More than 4,000 works of art, including works by Aboriginal & Torres Strait Islander artists, are on display.

It displays many art styles and techniques through a permanent collection and frequently changing temporary exhibitions.

207

Every day, optional, no-cost guided tours are offered. The MCA Café is located indoors and provides contemporary Australian food in addition to lovely views of Sydney Harbour.

Location: *The Rocks, NSW 2000, Australia, 140 George St.*

Open: *Wednesday through Monday, 10 am to 5 pm (Tuesdays closed).*

Phone: +61 (0)2 9245 2400

3. Australian Museum

One of the oldest museums in the country

Excellent for: • History • Families • Budget

One of Australia's first museums, the Australian Museum, was established in 1827. Its extensive zoological and anthropological collections, totaling more than 21 million items and specimens, are included in its permanent displays.

Since admission to the Australian Museum is free all year long, anyone can visit. The children's activities and Prehistoric Playground may be appealing to families. It provides excellent nighttime entertainment for individuals who wish to learn about the natural world while they are visiting Sydney and has late operating hours on Wednesday.

Location: 1 William St, Australia (2010), Darlinghurst, NSW

Open: Thursday through Tuesday, 10 am to 5 pm, and Wednesday, 10 am to 9 pm

Phone: +61 (0)2 9320 6000

4. Powerhouse Museum

A state-of-the-art science museum

Good for: • History • Families • Budget

A contemporary museum with an emphasis on innovation, science, and design is called The Powerhouse Museum. It is located in a historic electric tram that has been renovated in Sydney's Ultimo neighborhood, around 750 meters south of Darling Harbour. More than 500,000 objects from Australian social history, science, technology, transportation, and space exploration are on display at the museum.

Temporary displays of Indigenous heritage, photographic exhibits, fashion shows, and Australian transport history are among the topics covered. The museum offers guided tours for persons with special needs, and admission is free.

Location: *Ultimo, NSW 2007, Australia, 500 Harris St.*

Open: *Friday through Wednesday, 10 am to 5 pm, and Thursday, 10 am to 9 pm.*

Phone: +61 (0)2 9217 0111

5. Hyde Park Barracks

A former prison turned UNESCO-listed museum

Good for: • History • Families

In the heart of Sydney, the Hyde Park Barracks is a UNESCO World Heritage site. The former prison provides information on Australia's past as a penal colony, the effects it had on Aboriginal people, and later immigration patterns. More than 4,000 authentic artifacts are on display, and interactive audio technology is used to lead visitors through the museum.

During a visit, you can trace the steps of actual prisoners and learn about their unique experiences and possessions. It's a unique chance to gain more accurate knowledge of Australia's colonial past. The Hyde Park Barracks has an entrance price, but there are discounts available for families, kids, and concessions.

Location: Macquarie St. and Queens Square, Sydney, NSW 2000, Australia

Open: Thursday through Sunday, 10 am to 5 pm (Closed: Monday through Wednesday)

Phone: +61 (0)2 8239 2311

6. Art Gallery of New South Wales

Classical art gallery featuring modern and Aboriginal art

Good for: • History • Families • Budget

Contemporary, historical, and indigenous artwork are on show at the Art Gallery of New South Wales. It is located in a compound with a classical design on Sydney Harbour and was founded in 1871. It now occupies two buildings united by a public garden as a result of its development.

Despite being one of Australia's top art institutions, admission is free, allowing just about anyone to discover the regional art scene. You can discover a variety of art media and eras, such as modern and Aboriginal art, through numerous exhibitions.

Free daily guided tours are available, and Wednesday nights feature free plays, movies, and other activities.

Location: Sydney, Australia (NSW 2000), Art Gallery Road

Open: Thursday through Tuesday, 10 am to 5 pm, and Wednesday, 10 am to 10 pm.

Phone: +61 (0)2 9225 1700

7. Museum of Sydney

A museum that celebrates this Australian city

Good for: • History • Families • Budget

One of the most varied museums in Australia is the Museum of Sydney. Circular Quay is close by, making it simple to get there from the city center. This venue, which is a part of the Sydney Living Museums collection, was constructed on the site of Australia's first government house to honor the history and culture of the area.

The museum hosts a changing roster of displays and activities that explore the state's colonial past as well as Aboriginal culture and history. It employs a variety of media, including photography, movies, and art displays, to highlight the city. There is no cost to enter.

Location: *Sydney, NSW 2000, Australia, Cnr. Bridge St. & Phillip St.*

Open: *Daily from 10AM to 5PM*

Phone: +61 (0)2 9251 5988

8. The Rocks Discovery Museum

Discover the history of a local landmark.

Excellent for: • History • Families

The Rocks Discovery Museum is a fantastic resource for learning about Sydney The Rocks neighborhood's history. The museum, which is housed in three structures that date back to 1844, uses artifacts found during archaeological digs to chronicle the history of the waterfront district from pre-colonial times to the present.

A fascinating virtual tour will guide you through the stories of the region and the effects of European settlement in the four permanent display rooms. It places a lot of focus on using artifacts and images to depict local Aboriginal history. Families and school field trips are particularly well-liked for educating younger generations about the local history.

Location: *The Rocks, NSW 2000, Australia, Kendall Ln*

Open: *Daily from 10AM to 5PM*

Phone: +61 (0)2 9240 8680

9. The Mint

One of Australia's oldest remaining public structures.

Good for: • History • Families • Budget

One of Australia's oldest still-standing public structures is Sydney's Mint. It was formerly a section of Governor Macquarie's prisoner hospital and eventually developed into the first Royal Mint location outside of London. The Caroline Simpson Library and the Research Collection, the Bullion Café, and a public area available for rental are currently housed in the former coin foundry.

It's not much of a museum in terms of conventional exhibits and displays, but it's a well-liked destination for anyone who is interested in historic structures and colonial architecture. Many of the interior rooms are still in good condition, providing insight into the building's past. Entry to The Mint is free all year long.

Location: *10 Macquarie Street, Sydney, Australia, 2000*

Open: *Monday through Friday, 9AM to 4PM (weekends closed)*

Phone: +61 (0)2 8239 2288

- **Justice and Police Museum**

Discover the dark side of Sydney's underworld

Good for: • History • Families

The Justice and Police Museum, housed in a police station from the 1890s, focuses on Sydney's troubled past. It's among the finest ways to discover the background of crime, law enforcement, courts, and unlawful behavior. You can discover information on infamous criminals like gangs, smugglers, and bushrangers through an impressive database of images and artifacts.

Even the holding cells, offices, charge rooms, and courts from the 1890s may be seen to gain a sense of Sydney's long history of the criminal underworld. The Justice and Police Museum, which is only open on weekends, is conveniently located next to Circular Quay.

Location: *Sydney, NSW 2000, Australia, Cnr. Phillip and Albert Streets*

Open on weekends from 10 am to 5 pm.

Phone: +61 (0)2 9252 1144

10 Best Foods to Eat In Sydney

The best Australian food in Sydney is arguably the best food in the entire world since it is made with the city's signature flair. And while it's true that Sydney, Australia's largest city, offers delicious cuisine from all over the world, there are still a few traditional Australian dishes you should seek out while there. The avocado, a hipster favorite, is featured here, along with a wide variety of amazing seafood from the abundant Pacific Ocean off the coast.

1. Barramundi

In restaurants all around Australia, barramundi is a traditional fish dish, although Sydney is where you'll find it most frequently. The barramundi is a resilient species that is native to Australia and the Indo-Pacific. They can be raised without the use of hormones or antibiotics and naturally contain high levels of heart-healthy Omega-3 fatty acids.

They have a moderate flavor and a toothsome texture and are an excellent source of lean protein. It's also very hard to overcook them. Similar to popular whitefish varieties, barramundi has a mild flavor and can also be used in a variety of dishes.

2. Sydney rock oyster

A gourmet gem of the Australian coast is the Sydney rock oyster. The Sydney rock oyster has a very deep, rich, and enduring sweetness that sets it apart from other oyster species, despite the fact that its flavor might vary depending on its location. It can be consumed raw, roasted, or shallow-fried in a light batter for seasonal or regional subtleties. It has a mineral intensity and a finish that resembles copper.

With quality wine or bacon and Worcestershire sauce, which brings out the saline notes that match the fatty richness of cured pig, Sydney rock oysters' different flavors go well together.

3. Australian prawns

A profusion of luscious seafood is brought by the warm weather and year-round sunshine, including sweet, juicy prawns that come in several types with distinctive flavors. King prawns may be prepared in a variety of ways and have a sweet, rich flavor and moist flesh that makes them ideal for a cocktail dish with dipping sauces.

With a mild flavor and a stunning appearance, tiger prawns are a delectable species that is frequently used in soups or served with mayonnaise or aioli. For casseroles, paellas, and laksas, the majority of prawn species taste wonderful battered, crumbed, or used in tempura dishes.

4. Avocado on toast

Avocado is a wholesome ingredient found in many Australian cuisines, particularly those for breakfast. For an alternative to margarine or butter for a morning dose of fat and flavor, avocado is frequently mashed onto 1, 2, or 3 slices of toasted, crusty bread.

For a distinctive flavor combination, avocado may be paired with feta cheese, sesame seeds, olive oil, or poached eggs in some spreads. Additionally, you might get avocado on toast with beetroot and black sesame hummus, which will enhance the flavor and nutritional value of your morning.

5. Bacon and egg roll

Breakfast of bacon and eggs is a British custom that has affected Australian mornings, but the dish has evolved into a take-along breakfast treat that is particular to the city or region. The bacon and egg roll is frequently served in Sydney with fresh tomato relish, caramelized onions, and artisan bread rolls stuffed with grains or seeds. On freshly baked bread, they can also be packed with fried eggs and smoky bacon. The bacon and egg roll, no matter how it's made, is a classic breakfast item that combines healthy ingredients with regional flavors for a filling, hearty breakfast.

6. Lamington cake

The Lamington is a popular local treat that many people believe to be Australia's national cake. It's a soft, sweet square of sponge cake that's been doused in rich chocolate sauce and covered in flaky coconut.

Bakeries use inventive variations on the traditional recipe to create a variety of cakes that include lamingtons. Some bakeries prefer to top their desserts with salted caramel or dulce de leche for a decadent treat or add jam then cream to the center for a sweeter flavor with richer texture.

7. Potato cake

Many Australians adore fried potato cake, a traditional staple known for its thick, crispy outside and fluffy interior. Fried potatoes are suitable for any meal because of their mild flavors, which also go well with a number of other ingredients, including smoked salmon, eggs, and avocado.

Fried potato cakes are sometimes served with fish and chips in some restaurants and takeaways, frequently with the same batter recipe to enhance the flavor.

8. Yellowfin tuna

Although yellowfin tuna is frequently used in sashimi and sushi, its high abundance in Australian seas makes it one of the most well-liked fish in Sydney and some of Australia's best cuisine. Yellowfin tuna is an excellent fish to eat raw since it has a mild, meaty flavor, similar to that of steak, and bright-red, firm, moist, and flaky meat.

Yellowfin tuna cutlets and steaks can be grilled, baked, smoked, poached, marinated, or barbecued. They typically taste best when the outside is seared, and the interior is left red. The flavor of yellowfin becomes considerably more prominent when combined with potent flavors like burnt capsicum, balsamic vinegar, eggplant, wasabi, or bitter greens.

9. John Dory

John Dory is a well-liked fish kind that is suitable for a variety of fish recipes and is frequently found in the waters of Sydney Harbour. It has a firm, flaky texture, delicate white meat, and a mild, somewhat sweet flavor that goes well with a variety of conventional herbs, spices, and preparations.

Various regional flavors and vegetables can be added to John Dory before fish is steamed, poached, breaded and fried, baked, or sautéed. John Dory is appropriate for both classic fish and chips and fine-dining recipes since it is minimal in fat and has a buttery, melt-in-your-mouth texture.

10. Witchetty grub

The witchetty grub, a true indigenous staple, has been a regular dish eaten in Australia for thousands of years but is not something you'll find on most menus. Witchetty grubs can be cooked to produce a crisp, crunchy skin that is comparable to roasted chicken and a light-yellow interior that resembles a fried egg, while they can also be eaten raw and have a strong, nutty flavor.

It's also a meat substitute that's strong in protein and nutrient-dense. You can observe an indigenous person find and gather the grub to be eaten raw for the most genuine experience.

227

10 Best Beaches in Sydney

Numerous beaches can be found in and around Sydney, a city blessed with breathtaking coastlines that surfers and beach lovers adore. The beaches of Sydney truly have something for everyone, from the throngs of sun-kissed bodies strutting Bondi Beach to the surf-spectacular Manly Beach to the secluded stretches of sand found along the mountainous coastlines of protected national parks.

Locals who need a quick break from the hustle and bustle of the city cherish Sydney's best beaches, which are a must-see for tourists as well. The top 10 beaches in Sydney are listed below.

1. Bondi Beach

Bondi is a crowded beach with a lot to see and do, with smooth golden sands extending for a kilometer between two headlands. Bondi, located 8 kilometers from Sydney's CBD, is a paradise for surfing, swimming, sunbathing, and taking the ideal Instagram photo on the sand.

Swim in the picturesque Icebergs pool, which is perched over the beach and costs $6.50 to enter. Visit the Bondi Market every Sunday to find regional products, including handcrafted jewelry, vintage items, and crafts. There are many delicious restaurants in Bondi, including trendy cafes like Rocker, burger joints, bakeries, and establishments like Panama House that provide opulent brunches and cocktails.

2. Bronte Beach

Take your family to a park for a picnic.

Bronte Beach, located in Sydney's eastern suburbs about 3 km from Bondi Beach, is perfect for a family vacation thanks to its gentle sands and nearby park with barbeque facilities, a playground, and shaded spots to unwind. The breathtaking seaside rock pools on the southern headland can be enjoyed for free. Although there are fewer people surfing here than in Bondi, it is still better to leave the heavier swells to more seasoned surfers.

You can discover a number of cafes and restaurants on Bronte Road, including Bogey Hole Café, which specializes in handcrafted pastries and veggie burgers, and Three Blue Ducks, which serves contemporary Australian breakfasts and lunches.

3. Tamarama Beach

For the Sculpture by the Sea festival, go in late October.

Just a few hundred meters from Bronte Beach, on the coastal path, is this hidden treasure of a beach. Tamarama is only 80 meters long, yet it has beautiful, silky sand and excellent surfing waves. A playground, grilling pits, and a café are located in the nearby park.

Tamarama is known as "Glamarama" since it is a popular destination for attractive individuals. One would be shocked to find that in the late 1800s, an amusement park with an elephant ride and a roller coaster was located on Tamarama's immaculate shoreline. Pay attention to the lifeguards' warnings because Tamarama might occasionally be unsafe for swimming.

4. Coogee Beach

A great area to snorkel and swim

Coogee is a 400-meter stretch of smooth sand with quiet surf and a charming promenade with interesting gardens and historic structures. The Bondi to Coogee route, which runs 6 kilometers up the coast, is a beautiful way to get around here. At the beach's ends, you can find rock pools such as Wylie's Baths, which has a wooden platform, and the Ladies Baths, which are to the south.

Families enjoy going to the beach because there is lots of room for the kids to run around on the Grant Reserve playground and lawns. Before perusing the boutique stores on Arden Street, which runs parallel to the shore, get some fish and chips or ice cream from one of the cafes there.

5. Marley Beach

Get away from everything

A journey to Marley Beach is certainly worth the effort for anyone who has ever imagined taking a solitary stroll along the dunes. With its crystalline waters, sheer cliffs, and undulating sand dunes, Marley Beach in Royal National Park, less than an hour's drive south of Sydney, is a vision of untamed beauty.

Take the route from Bundeena to reach here, then stroll for about 4.5 kilometers along the lovely coastline path. A further 20-minute stroll will bring you to Little Marley Beach. Because of the high currents and lack of beach patrols, swimming is not recommended.

6. Manly Beach

The hub of the surfing community in Sydney

Manly, which is only a 30-minute ferry journey from Sydney's Circular Quay, is a great place to relax by the beach and meet locals. The Australian Open of Surfing is held in February at

Manly, one of the best surfing beaches in the city. Watch the surfers at work while you unwind on the dunes, or improve your wave riding technique by enrolling in lessons at one of the nearby surf shops.

Walk to The Corso strip, a vibrant pedestrian street dotted with dozens of stores, outdoor dining establishments, pubs, and art galleries, for a respite from the beach.

7. Shelly Beach

The best location for diving and snorkeling

Shelly Beach, a little but stunning beach in Sydney's Northern Beaches, can be found close to Manly. If you walk for around 15 minutes along the shore from the surf club in the southernmost part of Manly, you'll be rewarded with breathtaking vistas. Bring your snorkeling gear so you can explore the crystal-clear waters of this small cove within Cabbage Tree Bay's marine reserve.

In order to ride the renowned shallow-breaking surf wave known as "The Bower," surfers typically head to the western side of the beach. The beach features a restaurant called Le Kiosk and barbeque amenities.

8. Nielsen Park

Build sandcastles at Shark Beach

Nielsen Park, a tranquil beach retreat with a wide variety of amenities, is located in the Vaucluse neighborhood of Sydney's eastern suburbs. The park, which is bordered by Shark Beach, includes shady picnic spaces and a lovely walking path along the foreshore.

The shallow, quiet waters here are ideal for swimming and kayaking exploration. After dining at Nielsen Park Cafe, move on to Bottle and Glass Point to find a piece of shaded grass and take in the stunning views of Vaucluse Bay.

9. Milk Beach

Outstanding views of Sydney Harbour

Milk Beach, a small beach in Sydney's eastern suburbs, is ideal for a peaceful getaway. Milk Shore in Hermit Bay is a pleasant place for swimming, snorkeling, fishing, and exploring the rock formations at the edge of the shore. Milk Beach fronts the grounds of the historically significant Strickland House. Stay around later in the day to take in views of Sydney's skyline as it sets.

Although there are no amenities at this beach, Shark Beach in Nielsen Park, which includes picnic sites and restrooms, is only a 15-minute walk away. Enjoy the breathtaking seaside views by hiking the Hermitage Foreshore route.

10.Freshwater Beach

The birthplace of surfing in Australia

Freshwater is a popular beach destination for swimmers, surfers, and families in Sydney's Northern Beaches, located north of Manly Beach. Famous Hawaiian surfer "Duke" Kahanamoku visited the beach in 1915, where he inspired Australians to take up surfing by dazzling bystanders with his board-riding prowess.

At the northern end of the beach, there is a rock pool where you can swim laps. In the adjoining reserve, there are grilling and picnic areas, as well as a playground. Throughout the summer, on Sundays, when the Surf Life Saving Club conducts its "nippers" beach safety program, the beach is busiest.

Chapter 5: Melbourne

Introduction to Melbourne

Melbourne

Melbourne is the state capital of Victoria in Australia. It is situated on the southeasterly coast near the head of Port Phillip Bay. With a population of more than 1,000,000, the center city, which has a population of around 136,000, serves as the hub of a sizable metropolitan region that is the most southerly in the globe. Its population is second only to Sydney in Australia, and the two cities, which differ in many ways due to geography and history, have a friendly rivalry.

Melbourne's flat terrain has resulted in the regular creation of a rectangular layout of streets, but the city also boasts many lovely parks and offers much that is interesting and varied for those with an eye for architectural detail and history. The soaring skyscraper of the center city and the quickly growing eastern suburbs illustrate Melbourne's reputation for conservatism and financial stability, qualities that have aided in its rise. Area Melbourne's statistical division covers 2,971 square miles (7,695 square km), the City of Melbourne 14 square miles (36 square km), and Inner Melbourne 33 square miles (86 square km). Pop. (2016) Melbourne Statistical Division: 4,485,211; Inner Melbourne: 591,679; City of Melbourne: 135 969.

Physical and human geography

The landscape

The city site

The city of Melbourne is located 30 nautical miles (55 kilometers) from the bay's narrow entrance at the northern end of Port Phillip Bay. Less than 390 feet (120 meters) above sea level is the altitude of most of the flat land. Melbourne's growth from its beginnings at the Yarra River's mouth to its current form shows a clear relationship with the terrain's geology and drainage. Basalt flows from the Cenozoic Era, or the last 65

241

million years, filled the preexisting valleys and produced flat, homogeneous plains west of the original city site. However, the eastern portion is made up of undulating and split-up beds of sandstones, shales, and conglomerates that were formed between 445 and 360 million years ago during the Silurian and Devonian periods. In comparison to the basalt plains, the eastern region's stronger soils and higher yearly rainfall supported a much denser cover of trees. It should not come as a surprise that the majority of Melbourne's development has occurred on the expansive areas of land east of Darebin Creek, between the Plenty and Yarra rivers, and between Koonung and Gardiner's creeks. While corresponding development on the west coast of the bay only stretches for 10 miles (16 km), Melbourne's urban growth today stretches along the entire eastern side of Port Phillip Bay, from the Yarra River's mouth to Point Nepean, 60 miles (97 kilometers) away.

Climate

Melbourne's weather is caused by high-pressure cells moving eastward and being split by low-pressure troughs. These patterns take a path that travels over northern Victoria in the winter and goes south of the continent in the summer. The 26 inches (660 mm) of annual precipitation falls over the course of the year fairly equally, with January typically being the driest and October typically the wettest. The average daily maximum temperature ranges from 55 °F (13 °C) in July to 79 °F (26 °C) in January. Temperatures are moderate, rarely dropping below freezing. Melbourne is protected from the severe air pollution that some other major cities experience thanks to winds associated with weather systems moving eastward.

View of Venice, Italy's principal waterway, the Grand Canal (Canale Grande in Italian), with gondolas on the water and houses lining the banks.

The city layout

The layout of Melbourne's original settlement, which now serves as the city's financial, legal, administrative, and ecclesiastical core, is still rectangular. The Yarra River frontage is present throughout the neighborhood. In addition to Victoria's Houses of Parliament, Anglican and Catholic cathedrals, venues for arts and entertainment, the Law Courts, museums, the State Library, and a number of financial organizations, such as the Melbourne Stock Exchange and also the headquarters of major banks, are all located within this core. Two important locations that serve as the area's hub are Bourke and Swanston Streets, which have been converted into pedestrian malls and are now off-limits to cars. The Town Hall, the Law Courts, and the Exhibition Building are remarkable examples of 19th-century government architecture, even though the majority of the city's structures are contemporary. The city is organized into 14 precincts, which are areas distinguished by concentrations of one or more ethnic groups, businesses, or tourist sites.

The first suburbs, including Brighton, Carlton, Collingwood, Richmond, Prahran, and St. Kilda, all have streets that are primarily rectangular in shape. Row homes, frequently with verandas adorned with iron lacework, were typical of the districts near the city's center. Some of these historic terraces have been maintained in Carlton and South Melbourne.

Iconic Landmarks and Attractions

Melbourne offers a wide range of sights to see and things to do, whether you want to get in touch with nature and hike through the stunning outback or lose yourself in the vibrant nightlife. The city's absolute greatest offerings are listed here. It can also be used as a starting point for your travel preparations.

What are the top things you can do in Melbourne?

1. National Gallery of Victoria

Admire an impressive collection of Aboriginal artworks

Good for:

• History

• Group

• Budget

The National Gallery of Victoria is the oldest and biggest art gallery in the nation. It was founded in 1861. The gallery was established in the 19th century's Gold Rush era, a time when demand for great art was at an all-time high.

The National Gallery has built up an amazing collection over time and, with that, a reputation to match. Over 70,000 pieces of authentic Australian Aboriginal art and post-colonial works make up its collection. It's recommended to stay the entire day here and to arrive early in the morning to beat the lines. After your visit, don't forget to stroll along the Yarra River on the Southbank to take in the sights.

Location: ***180 St. Kilda Road, Melbourne, Australia, 3006.***

Open every day from 10AM to 5PM

Phone: +61 (0)3 8620 2222

2. State Library Victoria

A historic center for learning and culture

Good for: History and Photo

Sir Redmond Barry established the State Library Victoria (SLV), a well-conserved state library in Melbourne, in 1856. This stunning, modern monument is a work of art in architecture that is completely operational. It was initially intended to hold a library, museum, and gallery, but it has since undergone numerous renovations to stay up with the times. You can study and do research, or you can just take in educational and cultural events.

There are breathtaking architectural elements, works of art, works of literature, sculptures, artifacts, and activities everywhere you turn, even if you're not a reader. The La Trobe Reading Room and Dome Galleries should not be missed; when it was finished in 1913, its enormous and spectacular domed ceiling was the largest in the world.

Address: 328 Swanston St, Melbourne, Australia, 3000

Open every day from 10:00 am to 6:00 pm.

Phone: +61 (0)3 8664 7000

3. Melbourne laneways and arcades

Uncover endless street art along cobbled walkways

Good for: History, Photo, and Budget

Vibrant street art is everywhere, covering the laneways and arcades that are so characteristic of Melbourne. Despite Melbourne's impressive Victorian arcades and lovely cobblestone streets, it is the city's thriving art culture that truly makes Melbourne a delectable feast.

Hosier Lane, a charming alley famed for its changing street art, is the most well-known of these. Market Lane, a fragrant entrance to the city's famous Chinatown, and Block Arcade, where elegant French Renaissance architecture frames fashionable stores like Georg Jensen and Crabtree & Evelyn, are other locations worth mentioning.

4. Federation Square

Explore this popular plaza rife with culture

Good for: History, Photo, Budget, and Group

Located in the center of the city, Federation Square is a well-known landmark where throngs of people congregate for everything from meals to coffee. This 2002-opened cultural center is home to numerous stores, eateries, pubs, a museum, an art gallery, and an auditorium.

If you have the time, you should definitely visit the Ian Potter Center. In 20 galleries at this art museum, there are some outstanding exhibits of Indigenous and non-Indigenous works of art from the colonial era to the present. If you have the time (and the stamina), cross the river to the International Gallery, which has hosted shows from renowned museums, including the MOMA in New York. Walking in comfy footwear is highly encouraged.

Location: *Melbourne, VIC 3000, Australia, Swanton Street & Flinders Street*

5. Melbourne Skydeck

Unsurpassed views of the city and beyond
Good for: Couples, Photos, and Group

With a height of 285 meters, the Melbourne Skydeck provides the Southern Hemisphere's tallest public viewing platform. In the Australian state of Victoria, the main city has spectacular views. Binoculars and viewfinders are available on the largely enclosed 360-degree viewing deck to assist you in identifying notable landmarks and other features. There is a small outside space called The Terrace that may be closed if the winds are too strong if you wish to monitor the weather up here.

While you're up here, see The Edge for a spectacular experience. This building's protruding 3-meter glass cube gives you the impression that you are hovering nearly 300 meters above Melbourne's downtown streets.

Location: *Southbank, VIC 3006, Australia, 7 Riverside Quay*

Open: Sunday through Thursday from noon to 9 pm and on Friday and Saturday from noon to 10 pm.

Phone: +61 (0)3 9693 8888

6. Melbourne Zoo

One of the most popular wildlife sanctuaries in Australia

Good for: Families

More than 320 kinds of animals from all over the world are housed in the Melbourne Zoo, where they are displayed in various displays and bioclimatic zones. It has a variety of habitats, including the Gorilla Rainforest (home to gorillas and lemurs), the Trail of the Elephants (home to elephants, orangutans, and tigers), and an Australian bush area where visitors may see koalas, kangaroos, wombats, and other native animals.

Non-member entry tickets are available online and must be reserved in advance. On weekends and a few holidays, children under 16 are admitted free of charge. Being one of Australia's oldest animal sanctuaries, Melbourne Zoo has been around for more than 160 years.

Elliott Avenue, Parkville, Australia, 3052

Open every day from 9:00AM to 5:00PM

Phone: *+61 (0)1300 966 784*

7. Royal Botanic Gardens

Enjoy gorgeous displays of wildlife

Good for: Couples, Families, and Photo

The Royal Botanical Gardens, which were first established in 1846, include approximately 87 acres of groomed gardens and over 10,000 different species of plants and animals. You can decide to come here for the day's final rays of sunshine after exploring the city, or you can spend a leisurely day strolling the lovely green gardens and stopping to lie on the grass and enjoy the sunshine.

The gardens are a short 30 km drive or rail ride from the city's central business district. To guard from the intense Australian sun, don't forget to pack a hat and some sunscreen.

Location: South Yarra, VIC 3141, Australia, Birdwood Avenue

Open: *Daily from 7.30 am to 7.30 pm.*

Phone: *+61 (0)3 9252 2300*

8. Melbourne's markets

Shop for local produce and street food

Good for: Food, History, and Budget

Melbourne's markets are nothing short of magnificent, as it is quickly becoming Australia's food center. The bustling Queen Victoria Market, which has served as a cemetery, a livestock market, and a wholesale fruit and vegetable market, is the most well-known of them all.

The market is now a bustling community hub with entire halls devoted to organic foods, meats, cheeses, and handcrafted items. It even transforms into a cozy night market in the winter. Preston Market, which features a variety of ethnic options like Greek and Italian delis and bakeries as well as vendors selling one-of-a-kind handmade goods, is another market building a name for itself. Go to The Rose St. Artists' Market for the hippest vibes possible.

- **Great Ocean Road**

See multiple iconic sights within this stunning drive

Good for: Couples, Families, Photos, and Adventure

The Great Ocean Road is an amazing, apparently endless piece of road that runs through the countryside of the area, with the Ottaway Ranges and the coast at your sides. Start your journey at Torquay, and don't forget to stop in Lorne.

The Twelve Apostles, huge monoliths rising from the ocean's depths with their thinning foundation just a wave away from collapsing, the Gibson Steps, the London Arch, Bells Beach, and Logan's Beach are just a few of nature's heavyweights you can encounter along this 250 km-long natural wonder. For those who love to surf, keep an eye out for the World Surfing Championship, which considers Bells Beach to be a top surfing location. You might even see a humpback whale giving birth on Logan's Beach if the stars are in your favor.

- ## St. Kilda Beach

Soak in the sunshine on a lively beach

Good for: Couples, Families, Photo, and Budget

Melbourne's St. Kilda Beach is a well-known beach that is well-known for its colorful bathing boxes, which have given it some Instagram fame. However, aside from that, the beach is great for water sports like windsurfing, rollerblading, and beach walks or runs.

Some people believe that if you don't visit St. Kilda Beach, you truly haven't really been to Melbourne. As you people-watch under your billowing parasol, you'll quickly realize that this is the place to be for some lively beach action. Arrive early to secure a decent place on the sand and set up your headquarters for the day.

Australia's St Kilda Foreshore, St Kilda, VIC 3182

- ## Phillip Island

Spend the sunset with hundreds of tiny penguins

Good for: Couples, Families, and Photo

Phillip Island, which is located on the fringes of the city, is a haven for nature enthusiasts. Just before evening falls, visit the island's shoreline to witness the breathtaking sight of hundreds of small penguins returning from a busy day at sea. They can be seen on Summerland Beach and will cutely waddle to their homes.

If you still feel like you need more nature, visit the island's wildlife park, where you can see koalas, seals, dolphins, wallabies, and kangaroos. This is a fantastic family activity day that will keep the kids entertained and happy. On the island, tours are offered for people who prefer a more educational visit.

- **Melbourne rooftop bars**

Look out over city lights with a cocktail in hand

Good for: Nightlife and Group

The best rooftop bars in the nation, in my opinion, are in Melbourne. Despite the city's reputation for unpredictable weather, It can be incredibly lovely when the sun is out.

The Rooftop at QT is the place to go if you want to enjoy some sunshine and alcohol. One of the biggest rooftop bars in the city, it also offers crowd-pleasing snacks like lobster rolls and fresh oysters.

Snappable views of the city's ever-expanding skyline are available here. Hipsters will swoon over The Rose St. Artists' Market, which has another gorgeous rooftop bar.

257

Chapter 6: Brisbane

Introduction to Brisbane

Brisbane, the state's capital, is a sizable metropolis and Australia's third-most populous city after Sydney and Melbourne. Aboriginal Australians have lived in this region for at least 22,000 years; it is estimated that they numbered between 6,000 and 10,000 when European settlers arrived in the 1820s.

The Brisbane River, which the city spans and was named after Sir Thomas Brisbane, the previous governor of New South

Wales, is the source of the city's name. The city was initially established in 1824 as a penal colony for repeat offenders from the Sydney colony. In 1842, the area became free to settle after the arrival of Christian missionaries.

When Queensland broke away from New South Wales in 1859, Brisbane was chosen as the state's capital. By the late 19th century, it had developed into a significant port city and a hub for immigration.

Brisbane is a well-known international tourist destination and a significant transportation hub today. The Brisbane River meanders through the city's center on its way to the azure Moreton Bay, giving the area the nicknames "River City" and "Brissie" in current parlance. These nicknames serve to largely compliment the city's contemporary high-rise architecture and lush vegetation. Brisbane Botanic Gardens are located on Mt. Coot-tha, which towers over the city.

Numerous sites of historical, cultural, and architectural significance may be found in the area, including:

King George Square, a local historical landmark since 2004, is the site of several public gatherings, outdoor markets, and, most significantly, the 1930s-era Brisbane City Hall, one of Australia's most elaborate and stunning city halls. The Brisbane Museum is located on the third floor of the structure;

Queen Street Mall, the city's main shopping area and the core of the Central Business District of Brisbane, is bustling with activity;

Brisbane Arcade, a sizable shopping center housed in a magnificent old structure;

- General Post Office Building, a charming historical building that has been in operation since 1872;

- The Cathedral of St. Stephen, a Gothic Revival building constructed between 1863 and 1989;

- Old Government House, one of Brisbane's oldest structures, was built in 1862;

The Goodwill Bridge is a footbridge over the Brisbane River that serves as both a means of transportation and a piece of art.

Iconic Landmarks and Attractions

- **Brisbane Powerhouse**

Unquestionably one of the coolest sites in town, the Brisbane Powerhouse is located on the banks of the Brisbane River between Powerhouse Park and New Farm Park. Its interior, which once housed an abandoned power plant and was covered in graffiti, is now home to a variety of diverse cultural events, with something new happening every day.

It is a really distinctive and atmospheric location to see a performance, see a play, or peruse one of its outstanding art exhibitions, with remnants of industrial machinery scattered about. The Brisbane Powerhouse offers two fantastic eateries for you to try out in addition to its jam-packed schedule, which also includes stand-up comedy and theater acts, as well as stunning views of the river.

- ## Queensland Cultural Centre

The bustling arts and culture sector of the city beats at the Queensland Cultural Centre, which is only a short stroll from the CBD. Many of Brisbane's most significant and prestigious cultural institutions are located here, on the South Bank of the river, surrounded by gorgeous subtropical plants and gardens.

These include the Queensland Performing Arts Center, Queensland Art Gallery, and Queensland Museum. These are all housed in eye-catching structures with beautiful architecture.

The most well-known of these, however, is, without a doubt, the outstanding Gallery of Modern Art, both nationally and internationally. The Queensland Cultural Center is the ideal location to visit if you want to attend an art exhibition, discover more about Queensland, or take in a ballet or theatrical performance because of its many award-winning venues.

- ## City Botanic Gardens

One of Brisbane's most tranquil and enjoyable areas is the City Botanic Gardens, which are situated on a river bend. A wide variety of subtropical plants border its immaculate lawns, and some wonderfully natural rainforest is also on display. The tops of skyscrapers can only be made out peeking up above the palm and fig trees, giving the area its calm atmosphere that draws both locals and tourists.

Crop gardens that were first established in the 1820s to feed the city's jail population are now a wonderful recreational area with sculptures and statues, along with a tiny cafe and picnic tables. It is highly recommended to take a Sunday stroll by the City Botanic Gardens to browse the riverbank market there.

- ## Museum of Brisbane

The Museum of Brisbane provides a fascinating look into the inner workings of this bustling metropolis and is full of fascinating and interactive exhibitions on the past, present, and future of the city.

It takes you on a quick journey through time, starting with the indigenous people who originally lived in the area and ending with what Brisbane might look like in the future.

Photographs, Paintings, and sculptures that depict the history of the city, its inhabitants, and its culture are among the 5,000 or so pieces on display. The Museum of Brisbane is located on the third floor of the town hall and frequently holds temporary exhibitions.

- **Wheel of Brisbane**

The Wheel of Brisbane, which rises to a height of 60 meters, offers breathtaking views of the city and the river below. The large Ferris wheel, which sits directly at the entrance to the South Bank Parklands, is clearly seen from a great distance away.

When it is beautifully illuminated against the night sky in the evening, it is especially menacing-looking. It takes just under 15 minutes to spin in the air-conditioned pods; from above, Brisbane appears to stretch out in all its glory.

- ## City Hall

The stunning City Hall structure, one of Brisbane's most significant and outstanding historic landmarks, was opened to the public in 1930 after construction began in 1920. Even though it previously stood taller than any other structure in the city, a number of skyscrapers now rise over its stout sandstone columns and soaring clock tower.

While the exterior is unquestionably some of the best in the city, the interior is no less stunning; on the third floor, the Museum of Brisbane is located next to a sizable foyer and auditorium. It offers daily tours of the clock tower and free concerts on a regular basis, so there are many ways to admire and discover this magnificent old structure.

- ## Botanic Gardens Mt. Coot-tha

These spectacular Botanic Gardens, the second to be founded after the City Botanic Gardens, were opened to the public in 1976 and are located at the base of Mount Coot-tha, the tallest mountain in the region. The garden is divided into various distinct areas, with fern and cactus houses next to a lagoon, a stretch of rainforest, bamboo groves, and other plant life.

Bonsai House and the magnificent Japanese Garden are only two of its many highlights. It's fun to stroll about, and there are interesting attractions like a stellar planetarium and the National Freedom Wall that honors the conclusion of the Second World War.

- **Gallery of Modern Art**

The Gallery of Modern Art, a division of the Queensland Cultural Center, is housed in a striking-looking structure on the banks of the Brisbane River. It is frequently ranked among the best museums in the country.

The museum, which is focused on modern and contemporary art, features works by Australian, Asian, and Pacific Islander artists and regularly hosts temporary exhibitions.

Its broad collection addresses a wide range of fascinating subjects, including activism, Aboriginal rights, and the environment, through a variety of media. Alongside videos and pictures, there are sculptures and paintings on display. With its cutting-edge and imaginative installations, the Gallery of Modern Art is a must-see for anybody interested in art.

- **Roma Street Parkland**

This lovely park is tucked away among the city's numerous tall structures and towers and is a wonderful location to unwind. The Roma Street Parkland is the largest subtropical garden in the city center of the world and has many lush rainforest, ferns, and water features, making it quite similar to Central Park in New York.

It was formerly a train station and became a park in 2001. Themed gardens are situated next to leisure spaces that feature exercise equipment, playgrounds, and BBQ places. The untamed yet groomed gardens are very tranquil to meander in and provide locals and visitors with a break from the bustle of the city.

- **Mount Coot-tha Lookout**

Mount Coot-tha, the highest mountain in the region, rises to a height of 287 meters and, in the local language, means "Place of Honey." It is a great area to go hiking because it is covered in a thick jungle. Although most visitors just drive straight to the top, there are numerous routes and trails that wind their way up the mountainside.

On top of the mount, there is a kiosk where you can order for food and drinks, as well as a magnificent viewing platform from where you can take in one of the best panoramas of Brisbane and its surroundings. It is open at all hours and is referred to as the Lookout, so it is definitely worth getting up early to watch the sun rise over the city or coming later in the day to view the mesmerizing sunset.

• **Lone Pine Koala Sanctuary**

The Lone Pine Koala Sanctuary must be visited during any trip to Brisbane if you want to have a truly authentic Australian experience. The sanctuary, which lies 12 kilometers from the city center, is home to a variety of Australian wildlife, including wombats, dingoes, platypuses, koalas, and kangaroos.

You may feed kangaroos, take pictures with koalas, and even take on the role of a keeper for a day, in addition to learning everything there is to know during one of the park's talks and presentations. Over 130 of the adorable little animals live inside the oldest and largest koala sanctuary in the world, which was established in 1927.

- **South Bank Parklands**

The South Bank Parklands, which are just across the river from Brisbane's central business district, is among the most well-liked locations in the city among locals and visitors. Fountains and plazas, as well as restaurants, cafes, and small street markets offering local arts and crafts, are scattered throughout the park's captivating mix of groomed lawns and dense rainforest.

The lovely Nepal Peace Pagoda and the Courier Mail Piazza, which regularly offers entertaining free events, are tucked away next to these many treasures.

A spectacular man-made lake called Streets Beach, the bougainvillea-covered Grand Arbour, and the lovely riverside promenade with its stunning views of the city are also features of the South Bank Parklands in addition to all of the above.

269

With so much activity, the area constantly has a bustling vibe. It is unquestionably a must-see while in Brisbane.

Outdoor Activities and Adventures

When you first come to Brisbane, the inhabitants' love of the outdoors is probably the first thing you notice about them. With 283 days of sunlight annually, it's understandable why we're all about adventures, barbecues, and secret trips to the shore. Queenslanders really adore being outdoors, and with so many things available locally, you should too.

Here are some of the top outdoor activities close to Brisbane City.

1. Explore the city's numerous markets

Many of the city's fresh food, fashion, and designers' markets are located in Brisbane City, South Bank, and the surrounding areas. Everybody can find something to enjoy. For your perusal, we've compiled a list of all the top marketplaces.

2. Queen Street Mall features live music

Did you know Brisbane has the biggest free live music program in Australia? Local, national, and international musicians perform for the city's shoppers and bystanders as part of the City Sounds Program. To coordinate your trip with a free performance in the city, check the schedule.

3. Picnic in the parklands

The best time of day to plan a picnic at the park with friends is in the late afternoon. Anzac Square, Post Office Square, the Brisbane City Botanic Gardens, Roma Street Parklands, River Quay, and South Bank Parklands are some of the places you may visit to enjoy the rich greenery that can be found between the city and South Bank.

4. Ride the City Hopper

Get on board and experience the wind in your hair. You can travel between events at North Quay, South Bank 3, Holman Street, Maritime Museum, Thornton Street, Eagle Street Pier, Dockside, and Sydney Street terminals by using the free Brisbane City Hopper service. Every day of the week, from 6 a.m. until midnight, ferries run every 30 minutes.

5. Stroll along the city's Riverwalk

Experiencing indoor cabin fever? For some fresh air and views of the river, take a leisurely stroll along the city's Riverwalk. Go to Eagle Street Pier and proceed north toward New Farm Park to get there. If you run out of steam, take the City Hopper back from the Sydney Street terminal at New Farm.

6. Saturday night cocktails by the Brisbane River

Brisbane's balmy, sunny afternoons make for the ideal outdoor setting. That, plus a view and a couple of beers, equals pure heaven. On a bright afternoon, we advise you to go to Eagle Street Pier or Howard Smith Wharves and find a seat at Customs House, Riverbar, Felons, or Mr. Percival's for a view of the Story Bridge. Every Saturday and Sunday from 4 to 10 p.m., Howard Smith Wharves also organizes Weekends on the Lawn, which features live entertainment, food, beverages, and lawn games. Puppy watching is a must because fuzzy companions are always welcome.

7. Paddle a kayak with Riverlife.

What outdoor pursuits are more popular than swimming? This is a typical Brisbane experience and a lovely opportunity to see the river and the city at their most attractive. If you want a spectacular view of the city lights, check out the sunset paddles. This site offers online booking.

8. South Bank's Green Jam Sessions

Every Friday at 5.30 p.m., local performers perform free live jazz, folk, and modern rock music on Melbourne Street Green (outside QPAC). The Queensland Conservatorium Griffith University, JMC Academy, Jazz Music Institute, Brisbane City Council's The QUBE Effect, BrisAsia programs, and other organizations will benefit from your sponsorship.

9. Wandering Cooks offers a variety of meals.

Brisbane's culinary companies call this kitchen co-working space home, so it makes sense that it offers the public access to their delectable creations. The food changes every night because a different vendor is featured, and the bar is open every day until around 9 o'clock. Enjoy the tranquil ambiance in the courtyard close to South Brisbane's well-known Fish Lane.

10. Free fitness sessions in South Bank Parklands

The Medibank Feel Good Program offers free exercise classes at South Bank every day of the week. Classes range from vigorous energy and cardio workouts to more leisurely yoga and tai chi sessions. Everything is free; simply view the schedule online and like South Bank on Facebook to remain informed of changes to the class schedule.

11. Kangaroo Point Cliffs rock climbing

The ideal way to spend some time outside is to have a picnic at Kangaroo Point Cliffs, but why not earn your relaxing time by climbing the 20-meter-high weathered walls first? Utilize the time spent climbing to take in Brisbane's breathtaking views during the day or soak up the city's illuminations at night. The picnic will seem even more wonderful once you've completed the climb, we promise.

Chapter 7: Perth

Introduction to Perth

Perth is the state's capital and largest city. Perth is located along the Swan River's estuary, 12 miles (19 km) above its mouth, which forms the inner harbor of the nearby city of Fremantle. The fourth-largest city in Australia is the hub of a metropolitan area that is home to around three-fourths of the state's inhabitants.

The British decided to expand their settlement to that area and claim the entire continent at the beginning of the nineteenth century because they were wary of French and American interest in the Australian west coast. To select a town location, Captain (later Sir) James Stirling arrived in 1827. The land was taken over by Captain Sir Charles Fremantle the following year, and a colony with support from private investors was established in 1829. When it became a city in 1856, it was given the name of the Scottish county of Perth, where Sir George Murray, the then-secretary of state for the colonies, was born. It was telegraphed to Adelaide (in South Australia) in 1877, and the discovery of gold at Coolgardie-Kalgoorlie, 602 kilometers (374 miles) to the east, in 1890, as well as the opening of a better Fremantle harbor in 1901 and the completion of the transcontinental railroad in 1917, all provided significant growth spurts. In 1929, it was elevated to lord mayoralty.

View of Venice, Italy's principal waterway, the Grand Canal (Canale Grande in Italian), with gondolas on the water and houses lining the banks.

Heavy industries are centered in the suburbs of Kwinana, Fremantle, and Welshpool in Perth, a significant industrial hub. Paint, plaster, printed materials, sheet metal, cement, rubber, tractors, steel, aluminum, and nickel are among the diverse manufacturing products produced in the city. Additionally, there are facilities for processing food and refining petroleum. Particularly since Fremantle hosted America's Cup sailboat race in 1987, tourism has become more and more significant.

Eight months of the year, the city experiences a mild temperature; nevertheless, January and February are very hot, and both June and July are cool and moist. Numerous motorways, the transcontinental railroad, the Fremantle port, and the international airport all provide access to the city. The British Empire and Commonwealth Games (which are now known as the Commonwealth Games) were held there in 1962. Perth is home to cathedrals for both Catholics and Anglicans. University of Western Australia (1911), Curtin University of Technology (1966), Murdoch University (1973), Edith Cowan University (1991), and a campus of the University of Notre Dame Australia (1989) are among the universities in the Perth area. North Perth and Fremantle are home to a large Italian and

East and Southeast Asian immigrant population. Population: 1,445,078 in the Perth Statistical Division in 2006; 1,738,807 in the 2011 estimate.

Iconic Landmarks and Attractions

1. Cruise along the Swan River

According to local Aboriginals, "Waugal," the rainbow snake, created this twisting river. Both locals and visitors to Perth agree that it's the ideal location for outdoor entertainment.

Take a pleasant river trip between Perth and the old port of Fremantle to see some of the upscale homes in the riverfront areas. A trip up the river to the prosperous shores of Western Australia's Swan Valley, the oldest grape-growing region in the state, is another well-liked day trip. In these highly regarded restaurants, foodies may experience delectable handmade dishes and fresh local ingredients. From Barrack Square Jetty, the majority of ferries and river cruises leave.

Searching for different Swan River activities? Cast a line, cycle, hike, sail, swim, or kayak the tranquil waters. Enjoy a picnic in one of the riverside parks.

2. Bask on Perth's Beaches

Numerous stunning beaches are available in and near Perth for sun worshippers to choose from. One of Perth's most well-liked beaches, pine-fringed Cottesloe is closer than 15 minutes by car to the city center and features crystal-clear waves and a bustling café scene.

Another well-liked beach is Port Beach, and City Beach features a lot of picnic tables and a playground for kids.

Families should consider Rockingham Beach and the protected shore at Hillarys Boat Harbour, as well as the sheltered inlets on the winding Swan River like Como, Crawley, and Point Walter.

Prepared to catch some waves? One of Perth's best and most dependable surf breaks is at Trigg Point, while another excellent place to catch waves is at Scarborough.

Further away, the coasts of Rottnest Island and Penguin Island make for ideal family day trips and offer superb snorkeling.

3. Visit Elizabeth Quay.

Looking for things to do in the city center of Perth? Include Elizabeth Quay on your list of places to see. This brand-new waterfront pedestrian district, which is close to both the city center and the Swan River, is a popular destination for Perth nightlife.

If you're hungry, you can eat everything from delectable seafood specialties to gourmet burgers and pizza. Live music enhances the friendly atmosphere.

Going with the kids? At the BHP Water Park, they'll enjoy playing in the fountains, eating sour gelato, and riding the vintage carousel. The fountains light up in every color of the rainbow when you visit after dark. At the playground with a maritime theme, kids can also climb, jump, and "walk the plank."

A romantic place to wander along the sea is Elizabeth Quay. Along with the rocket-shaped Bell Tower, the Public Art Walk is decorated with outdoor sculptures and art installations. Along the way, you're greeted by lovely views of the city skyline and the ferry boats traversing the Swan River.

Looking for accommodations in Perth? Elizabeth Quay is a solid foundation. There is lodging in Perth available for every price level.

As the district grows, more attractions will be added, so if you're seeking fresh things to do in Perth, start here.

4. Visit the Perth Mint to get your money's worth in gold.

The Perth Mint is well-liked by both adults and kids and provides an interesting look into the past of gold in Western Australia. The world's heaviest coin, weighing a stunning one ton, as well as gold nuggets and bullion, are on show at the Gold Exhibition.

Watching pure gold being poured into a solid bar and admiring the largest collection of gold nuggets in the Southern Hemisphere are both possible in the 1899 melting house.

The tours include a brief film and hourly guided discussions that offer fascinating insights into the history of the Perth Mint and the discovery of gold in the state. One of the interesting things to do in Perth is to even calculate your weight in gold.

After your visit, browse the Argyle pink diamonds in the gift shop, buy a unique memento, or sit down for a Devonshire Tea in the café.

Location: In East Perth, Western Australia, at 310 Hay Street

Official site: http://www.perthmint.com.au

5. Hillarys Boat Harbour

Looking for family-friendly activities in Perth? Hillarys Boat Harbour is a sizable marina with eateries, shops, and family-friendly attractions located about 20 kilometers northwest of the city center of Perth.

Here, the biggest tourist attraction is the Aquarium of Western Australia. More than 200 kinds of marine life, including stingrays, manta rays, dolphins, and sharks, can be seen by strolling through an underwater glass tunnel.

This is a wonderful location for a pleasant family day out because of the bike routes, walkways, parks, and protected beaches. If you're looking for some inside family fun, Leisurezone has all your favorite vintage arcade games.

Do you want to go boating? From here, you can board a boat to Rottnest Island, one of Perth's favorite day adventures, as well as embark on fishing expeditions, whale-watching cruises, yacht charters, and dive excursions.

Location: Hillarys, Western Australia, 86 Southside Drive

Official site: http://hillarysboatharbour.com.au/

6. Art Gallery of Western Australia

The Art Gallery of Western Australia has a collection of both foreign and Australian art from 1829 to the present day and is located in the Perth Cultural Centre, about a minute's walk from the closest train station. The artwork from Australia and the Indian Ocean Rim is given particular attention.

The gallery features work by renowned artists, including Hans Heysen and Frederick McCubbin, in addition to a sizable collection of traditional and modern Indigenous art.

A renovation project is presently underway at the Art Gallery of Western Australia to provide a new rooftop event space with an outdoor sculpture path. Plans include two outdoor spaces with breathtaking views of Perth and a new interior gallery area for events and exhibitions.

Although admission to the gallery is free, a donation is requested at check-in, which art lovers will appreciate.

Address: *Perth Cultural Centre, James Street Mall, Perth, Western Australia*

Official site: https://artgallery.wa.gov.au/

7. Perth Zoo's Meet the Animals program

The Perth Zoo's lion

Perth Zoo, located around three kilometers from the city center, has delighted animal enthusiasts since 1898. In the Australian Bushwalk and Wetlands exhibitions, visitors from other countries can see some of the distinctive species of the nation. Kangaroos, koalas, wallabies, wombats, and Tasmanian devils are all present.

Other displays transport you to other ecosystems all over the planet. Visit the African Savannah to feed giraffes, the Asian Rainforest to admire orangutans, the Elephant Show to watch elephants perform, or the South American Primate Exhibit to observe pygmy marmosets.

Buses, cars, trains, bicycles, and ferries are all convenient ways to get to the zoo, and you may catch one at the Barrack Street Jetty.

Address: *In Perth, Western Australia, at 20 Labouchere Road*
Official site: http://perthzoo.wa.gov.au/

8. The Bell Tower

The Bell Tower in Barrack Square is one of the biggest musical instruments in the world, despite having the appearance of an extraterrestrial spacecraft or rocket. Despite having a futuristic appearance, it houses the historic 14th-century bells from Buckingham Palace's parish church in London, Saint Martin in the Fields Church.

Tickets for entry include both engaging exhibitions on the history of the bells and an interactive demonstration of the age-old craft of bell ringing.

Make sure to spend some time on the sixth floor's open-air observation deck to take in the 360-degree views of the city and Swan River while you're here. Couples in love can pay an additional price to put a customized "love lock" on a chain-link fence.

The Bell Tower is simple to get to. From the CBD, it takes roughly five minutes to walk here.

Elizabeth Quay, a brand-new riverfront district nearby featuring eateries, stores, cafés, and entertainment options, is close by.

Address: *Riverside Drive and Barrack Square in Perth, Western Australia*

Official site: https://www.thebelltower.com.au/

9. Find Inspiration at Scitech

Scitech is a fantastic addition to your plan for touring if you are traveling with unruly children. Through creative and interactive exhibits, this fun, family-friendly museum inspires children to investigate science, technology, engineering, and math.

Discoverland is specifically made for children aged three to seven. Displays on air, electricity, water, gravity, and magnets can be found here. Youngsters can dress up as marine creatures and crawl through a tunnel at the miniature aquarium exhibit, or they can use a periscope to spy on their parents in the construction zone.

Older children will love the planetarium movies, and science displays at Waterlandia, which covers the water cycle. A puppet theater and unique displays with a theme complete the entertainment.

Address: West Perth, Western Australia's City West Center, is located at the intersection of Sutherland Street and Railway Street.
Official site: http://www.scitech.org.au/

10.St. Mary's Cathedral

St. Mary's Cathedral
St. Mary's Cathedral is a tranquil location to get away from the city's bustle. This magnificent neo-Gothic church, which took three centuries to build, was dedicated in 1865 and underwent numerous renovations throughout the years. The original Perth plan from 1838 included the cathedral's future location.

Every Tuesday at 10:30 am, a tour of the cathedral is available for those who want to learn more about it. The church office across the street sells tickets. The church has an ethereal radiance at night, thanks to the lights.

Address: 17 Victoria Square, Perth, Western Australia

11. Aviation Heritage Museum

Aviation Heritage Museum

The intriguing exhibits in the Aviation Heritage Museum can surprise you, even if you have no interest in flying machines. Thousands of artifacts and more than 30 aircraft are on display in exhibits that cover both civil and military aviation. They follow the development of aircraft from two-winged World War I aircraft to modern passenger jets.

You can also reserve a private tour of a Lancaster bomber, a Dakota C-47, or a Spitfire Mark XXII for an additional cost.

South of Perth, the Aviation Heritage Museum is located around 15 kilometers away.

Address: *Bull Creek Drive, Air Force Memorial Estate, Bull Creek, Western Australia*

Official site: http://www.raafawa.org.au/museum/

Perth lodging options for sightseeing

The city center, close to the glistening Swan River, is one of the greatest places to stay for first-time visitors to Perth. Those who intend to take public transportation will find this to be extremely convenient. The Western Australian Museum, St. Mary's Cathedral, the Art Gallery of Western Australia, and Kings Park are just a short stroll away, as are fantastic shopping and dining options. Free CAT buses make looping stops at the city's biggest attractions. Some of the top hotels in this area are listed below:

- **Luxury hotel**

Steps away from fantastic shopping and St. Mary's Cathedral, in a lovingly restored mid-19th-century state building, COMO The Treasury combines contemporary styling in its large rooms with ornate architectural features. The holistic spa, gym, and indoor pool are among its contemporary features.

Elizabeth Quay's The Ritz Carlton, Perth, is a well-liked 5-star option that commands a view of the Swan River. Swim in the infinity pool with a river view, unwind in the lavish spa, and enjoy the views from the modern rooms' floor-to-ceiling windows.

Steps from the Perth Mint and a short stroll from Elizabeth Quay's shops and eateries, Pan Pacific Perth is a larger property in the heart of the city.

- **Mid-Range Hotels:**

The apartment-style Quest Mounts Bay Road, located at the base of Kings Park, is a fantastic choice for extended stays. The rooms, which vary from studios to one-bedroom flats to dual studio interconnecting apartments, are light and contemporary. There is no charge for guest laundry.

The popular 4-star Sage Hotel West Perth is located on the outskirts of the city and is only a short stroll from Kings Park. A pleasant stay is made possible with delicious meals and modern accommodations with incredibly comfy beds. Want to keep in shape? Exercise at the 24-hour fitness center or see Perth on a free loaner bike.

The European Hotel just steps away from stores, eateries, and St. Mary's Cathedral, is a favorite among guests for its hearty breakfast buffets and charming European decor.

- **Budget Hotels:**

The Comfort Hotel Perth City has spacious, spotless rooms at a good value and is close to the city's coastline, city center, and free CAT transport.

Baileys Motel in East Perth, which has a small pool and a family-run Italian/Mediterranean restaurant on-site, and the straightforward Citylights motel, which is near the city and public transportation, are further low-cost options in the CBD.

Chapter 8: Adelaide

Introduction to Adelaide

Adelaide is the state's capital and largest city. It is at the base of the Mount Lofty Ranges, about 9 miles (14 km) inland from the center of the eastern shore of the Gulf St. Vincent. It has a Mediterranean climate, with hot summers (average temperature in February is 74 °F [23 °C]) and mild winters (average temperature in July is 54 °F [12 °C]). On average, it rains 21 inches (530 mm) each year. The location was selected in 1836 by William Light, who served as the colony's first surveyor general. It sits on slightly sloping land along the

Torrens River, which separates it into a southern business sector and a northern residential area. Several large parkland areas separate the metropolis from its suburbs. It was formed as Australia's first municipal government in 1840 and given the name Queen Adelaide after the British King William IV's wife. However, the city council incurred significant debt and went out of existence in 1843. Following that, Adelaide was under the control of the provincial government until 1849, at which point a city commission was established. In 1852, a municipal corporation was reinstated, and in 1919, the city received a lord mayoralty.

The city's expansion was aided by the fertile surrounding plains, simple access to the Murray lowlands to the east and southeast, and the availability of mineral reserves in the close-by hills. Wheat, wool, fruits, and wine were all handled by this early agricultural marketing hub. Adelaide has since industrialized, with firms making chemicals, textiles, machinery, and vehicle parts thanks in part to its strategic location and fast access to raw materials. South of Adelaide, close to Port Noarlunga, a petroleum refinery was finished in 1962; a second refinery at Port Stanvac ran in the region until it was shut down in 2003. The Gidgealpa natural gas resources in northern South Australia's Cooper Basin are connected to Adelaide via pipeline. Adelaide, a hub for transportation by rail, sea, air, and road, receives the majority of the goods produced in the lower Murray River valley, which lacks a port near its mouth. Port Adelaide Enfield, located 7 miles (11 km) northwest of Adelaide, houses the city's own harbor facilities.

The Natural History Museum, the Adelaide Zoo, the Parliament and Government buildings, the University of Adelaide (established in 1874), and two cathedrals—St. Peter's (Anglican) and St. Francis Xavier's (Roman Catholic)—are notable municipal monuments. Flinders University was founded in the city in 1966, and the University of South Australia was founded there in 1991. The first international event of its sort to take place in Australia was the biennial Adelaide Festival of Arts (1960). Local government area population in 2006: 16,659; urban agglom. Population: 1,105,840.

Iconic Landmarks and Attractions

Adelaide, the capital of South Australia, has one of the highest standards of living in the world and is the fifth most populous city in Australia. The city, which is located on the south coast and borders the Gulf of St. Vincent, is frequently disregarded in favor of Sydney and Melbourne, but it is definitely worth a visit if you have the time. Adelaide, in contrast to many other Australian towns, was founded by free people who built a significant number of public spaces, wide boulevards, and numerous great churches.

The city now has a bustling restaurant scene that appeals to all palates as a result of the waves of immigrants that later came from all over the world. The outstanding institutions for arts and culture there are also appropriately multicultural in perspective.

This is reflected in the abundance of cultural occasions and festivals that Adelaide hosts throughout the year. The 'City of Churches' is a wonderful destination to spend some time, with many things to do in Adelaide and a highly cosmopolitan and affluent air about it.

1. St Peter's Cathedral

St. Peter's Cathedral, one of the most significant and well-known landmarks in the city, was established back in 1869. Two massive spires surround its stunning facade, which is evocative of the Cathedral of Notre Dame.

A beautiful rose window that closely resembles the one in Paris is located between them.

The cathedral is known for its stunning stained glass windows and enormous high altar, but it also has a sizable and potent organ that is utilized in regular services. St. Peter's has a long history of being well-known in the city for its outstanding choir and its frequent musical performances.

2. State Library of South Australia

The State Library of South Australia, housed in a magnificent ancient structure that was constructed during colonial times, will enchant book lovers and history buffs with its lovely, book-filled interior. Being the largest public research library in all of South Australia, it houses a sizable collection of books, images, audio, and visual materials on just about any subject imaginable.

The Mortlock Wing of the library, which is decorated in the French Renaissance style, is stunning from the exterior, but its interior truly steals the show; wrought-iron balconies stand in front of endless rows of softly lit books. The State Library, widely regarded as one of the most stunning libraries in the world, is well worth visiting if you're nearby.

3. Migration Museum

The Migration Museum is the ideal destination to visit if you want to learn more about Adelaide's and Australia's history, which have both been profoundly shaped by the numerous waves of immigrants that came to the nation.

The museum was established in 1986, and its extensive collection will transport you to a fascinating time period while illuminating the history of the state through objects, images, and narratives.

The museum offers several educational programs, is well-liked by both locals and visitors, and proudly promotes respect and tolerance for various cultures, peoples, and languages. Adelaide is known for its multiculturalism.

4. Waterfall Gully

Waterfall Gully is the spot to go if you want to get away from the bustle of the city. It is around five kilometers from Adelaide's downtown. The area's main draw is the dazzling waterfall known as "First Falls" in Cleveland Conservation Park, which is tucked away among the Mount Lofty Ranges' foothills.

Only the first, in a sequence of seven falls, rises to a height of around 30 meters, and the sight of its dazzling waters tumbling into the creek below is breathtaking. You can take a beautiful climb straight up Mount Lofty from here. You'll pass through several beautiful natural sites along the trip.

5. Rundle Mall

It's safe to say that Rundle Mall will satisfy all of your wants and needs with its over 800 stores, cafes, restaurants, and snack shops. The city's central pedestrianized shopping district is where you should go if you need to make any purchases. Chain retailers and Australian names coexist with independent boutiques and chic arcades. Rundle Mall features lovely statues, sculptures, and fountains, in addition to periodic, pop-up markets and stands that you can visit. Rundle Street and the streets surrounding it are the lifeblood of Adelaide.

6. South Australian Museum

The South Australian Museum, established in 1856, provides a fascinating look into the natural history of the country through engaging exhibitions on megafauna, mammals, meteorites, and fossils. You have access to an infinite number of galleries, as it contains over four million objects and specimens.

The world's largest collection of Aboriginal artwork and artifacts is kept there. The Aboriginal galleries are the main attraction, and many visitors travel from far and wide to learn more about their history and culture, despite the fact that there are also excellent exhibitions and displays on Ancient Egypt and Pacific Cultures.

7. Adelaide Zoo

Adelaide Zoo, the second-oldest zoo in the nation, which was established in 1883, is today home to more than 3,000 animals. The zoo is organized into different zones, such as Africa, Australia, and South America, and is situated close to the north of the city's core. All of the animals from those regions of the world live contentedly in their natural environments.

You can participate in a variety of seminars, presentations, and feeding sessions throughout the day, in addition to the educational and fascinating displays. Its two gigantic pandas, Wang Wang and Funi, who are presently on loan from China, are its principal attractions, in addition to its magnificent Sumatran tigers and fascinating orangutans.

Adelaide Zoo has over 300 unique species from around the world for visitors to see, making it a fun family outing.

8. Art Gallery of South Australia

The impressive collection of the Art Gallery of South Australia, which houses some 45,000 works of art, is a joy to peruse. The works of Australian artists are displayed alongside those of international artists.

It is the second-largest state art collection in the nation and is housed in a stunning edifice. It is recognized for its galleries of Australian, Aboriginal, & Torres Strait Islander artworks.

Its paintings, sculptures, photographs, and movies, which span 2000 years of history, are just breathtaking to look through. Highlights include the 20 bronze sculptures by Auguste Rodin and sketches by Hans Heysen. The gallery also organizes the yearly Tarnathi art festival, which features works by Aboriginal and Torres Strait Islander artists, as if all of that weren't enough.

9. Adelaide Botanic Garden

The Adelaide Botanic Gardens, located just northeast of the city center, is a tranquil and pleasant spot to spend some time and are great if you want to get close to nature. The gardens, which span a vast area, are divided into numerous distinct areas, where lush rainforest and tropical flora may be found alongside a lovely rose garden and some untamed wetlands.

It was founded in 1857 and had some amazing colonial architecture, with the Museum of Economic Botany and the lovely Palm House serving as the best examples. The stunning tropical foliage inside the Bicentennial Conservatory makes it especially worthwhile to visit. A charming little eatery is also located there.

10. Adelaide Oval

The Adelaide Oval, often regarded as the world's most beautiful cricket field, hosts numerous athletic events every year. The stadium, which was first used in 1871, still has some amazing Edwardian designs in certain locations, and its antique scoreboard helps it stand out among more contemporary construction.

A terrific way to see the fervor with which Australians support their home teams is to watch a game of cricket or Australian Rules football here. In addition to soaking in the enthralling and contagious mood of a game, guests can wander the charming grounds or climb up onto its enormous roof. You can see the lawn below and the surroundings from the top of its curved dome.

11. Adelaide Fringe

The Adelaide Fringe, the second-largest arts festival in the world after the Edinburgh Fringe Festival, brings the city to life with a variety of performances of music, art, and dance.

Over 7,000 artists from Australia and around the world participate in the festival, which runs from the middle of February to the middle of March and is spread out over hundreds of venues in Adelaide.

The range of different artworks on display is astounding. The Garden of Unearthly Delights is a fitting name for one of the primary locations. Every day of the month offers something fresh and unique to witness, from stand-up comedy performances to cutting-edge art installations, spontaneous theater plays, and circus extravaganzas.

12. Central Market

Adelaide's Central Market, located in the heart of the city, is bustling with activity. There are about 250 stalls there, selling anything from fresh seafood and veggies to local cheeses and wines. Various great cafes and eateries that nicely highlight the city's cosmopolitan nature are dotted among its various shops and booths.

While many locals also visit Central Market to shop or grab a bite to eat, It has always been a well-liked vacation spot due to the wide variety of food options and the astounding array of items and fresh fruit on display.

It has been in existence for 150 years and is one of the biggest covert markets in the Southern Hemisphere; the bustling atmosphere indicates that it will not slow down any time soon. One of the greatest venues in Adelaide to sample some of the amazing cuisines for which the city is so well known is Central Market, which is fun to meander through.

Accommodation IN ADELAIDE

Therefore, you won't have any trouble seeing everything Adelaide has to offer, regardless of the hotel you select.

Looking for the best accommodation options in Adelaide? We will discuss all available forms of lodging in Adelaide, from hostels to five-star hotels, as well as how to choose a place to stay in Adelaide in 2023.

The greatest places to stay in Adelaide, the cheapest places to stay in Adelaide, the best locations to visit in Adelaide, hotels near Adelaide attractions, a neighborhood guide to Adelaide, and much more are all shown in this chapter.

ADELAIDE CITY CENTRE - ADELAIDE CITY ACCOMMODATIONS FOR TOURISTS

The city center, also known as the central business district, is the best choice for first-time tourists or those with limited time in Adelaide because you'll be close to everything you want to see.

- The bulk of hostels in Adelaide are located in the CBD if you're looking for affordable hotels or other lodging.

307

- There are also a lot of luxurious and mid-range options available at the other end of the price spectrum.

- There are numerous cafes, restaurants (particularly near Rundle Street and the Adelaide Central Market), shops close to Rundle Mall, and the Adelaide Zoo in the city center, which is not just for business travelers.

Not sure where to stay in Adelaide's central business district? The city of Adelaide is rather tiny; From one end to the other, the trek takes 15 to 20 minutes.

While Rundle Mall and Rundle Street have a large number of eateries, cafes, and cocktail bars, Hindley Street is the nightlife hub with all the pubs and clubs. Compared to Hindley Street, Rundle Street is a tad more laid-back.

The Adelaide Fringe comes to town each February. At the end of Rundle Street, in Rymill Park, is where you'll find the Garden of Unearthly Delights.

Where to stay in Adelaide CBD

Cheapest backpacker hostels in the heart of Adelaide:

Adelaide Central YHA

Tequila Sunrise Hostel

Adelaide Travellers Inn Backpackers Hostel

Budget accommodation in Adelaide City Centre:

Adelaide Paringa

Adelaide Pulteney Motel

Quality Apartments Adelaide Central

Hotel Grand Chancellor Adelaide

Mid-range accommodation in Adelaide City Centre:

Ibis Adelaide

Crowne Plaza Adelaide, an IHG Hotel

Majestic Roof Garden Hotel

Hotel Indigo Adelaide Markets, an IHG Hotel

Family - Friendly accommodation in Adelaide City Centre:

Adelaide Rockford

Oaks Adelaide Horizons Suites

Quest on Franklin

Sofitel Adelaide

Affordable luxury lodging in Adelaide City Centre:

Pullman Adelaide

The Playford Adelaide – MGallery by Sofitel

Mayfair Hotel

Hilton Adelaide

InterContinental Adelaide, an IHG Hotel

Where Should a Family Stay in North Adelaide?

North Adelaide is the greater Adelaide neighborhood to choose for your vacation property if you want the ideal balance of city and nature.

You may enjoy plenty of open space in addition to the city, which is only a few minutes away. The River Torrens flows through this neighborhood, which also features beautiful cathedrals, old buildings, and mouthwatering food along O'Connell Street.

For a wonderful view of Adelaide during the day or at night, climb Montefiore Hill. The North region of Adelaide offers a wide selection of hotels due to the abundance of neighboring attractions.

Accommodations in North Adelaide

Affordable lodging in North Adelaide:

Comfort Hotel Adelaide Meridien

Princes Lodge Motel

Greenways Apartments

Econo Lodge North Adelaide

Mid-range accommodation in North Adelaide:

Majestic Tynte Street Apartments

Adelaide Inn

Majestic Minima Hotel

Fire Station Inn

Family - Friendly accommodation in North Adelaide:

Majestic M Suites

North Adelaide Boutique Stays Accommodation

Majestic Old Lion Apartments

Location: *Melbourne street views*

Accommodation in Adelaide for a City Break: Adelaide Hills

The Adelaide Hills region is situated immediately east of the city. Once you've arrived in the serenity of the hills, you won't believe you're only an hour from the large metropolis.

A fantastic starting point for exploring the adjacent woodlands, which are rich with animals and culture, are a number of charming hill towns.

Do you want to know where to stay in Adelaide Hills? In the towns of Hahndorf, Balhannah, Aldgate, Oakbank, and Stirling, there are numerous places to stay.

The farm-to-table philosophy used by many of the area's eateries will appeal to foodies. Even if you choose not to stay here, be sure to schedule a day trip to the Adelaide Hills. See our suggestions for chic lodging in the Adelaide Hills below.

Accommodations in Adelaide Hills

Affordable lodging in Adelaide Hills:

Discovery – Hahndorf Resort

Adelaide Hills' Camellia Cottage' – WiFi

Uraidla hideaway

Cook's Cottage in Balhannah

Mid-range accommodation in Adelaide Hills:

The Manna by Haus, Ascend Hotel Collection

Cladich Pavilions Bed and Breakfast

Aldgate Valley Bed and Breakfast

The Manor Basket Range

Family - Friendly accommodation in Adelaide Hills:

Amble at Hahndorf

Hahndorf Haven-Central Hahndorf

Holiday Haus Hahndorf – 4BR, Garden and Parking

Barristers Block Vigneron Villa

Affordable Luxury Lodge in Adelaide Hills:

Sequoia Lodge

Sticky Rice Villas

The Stirling Hotel

Mount Lofty House

Colorful autumn in Mount Lofty Adelaide Hills, South Australia

Accommodation in Adelaide to be near the beach? GLENELG.

Glenelg Adelaide is a fantastic option if you're looking for a great hotel outside of the city center. The finest lodging in Adelaide will be Glenelg for you if you are traveling with kids and intend to spend some time at the beach, gazing out into the South Pacific Ocean, or at playgrounds.

If you're trying to decide where in Adelaide to stay near the beach, what is the greatest option? Glenelg's vast, sandy beaches are ideal for relaxing, and Beachouse, an amusement park with rides, waterslides, and arcade games, will keep the kids occupied for hours.

Take the tram (public transportation) when you're ready to see more of downtown Adelaide; it will take you there in about 25 minutes.

Families and those who appreciate the outdoors might consider staying in Glenelg, which is also the best neighborhood in Adelaide! Our suggestions for lodging in Glenelg are listed below.

Accommodations in Glenelg Adelaide

Glenelg accommodations on a budget

Comfort Inn Glenelg

Taft Apartments

Atlantic Tower Motor Inn

Bay Motel Hotel

Mid-range accommodation in Glenelg:

Lights Landing Apartments

Glenelg Oasis Studios

Water Bay Villa Bed & Breakfast

The Heart of Glenelg

Family-Friendly Accommodation in Glenelg:

Oaks Glenelg Plaza Pier Suites

Ensenada Motor Inn and Suites

Nightcap at Watermark Glenelg

Belle Escapes -- Park View Family Stay at the Pier

Affordable Luxury Lodge in Glenelg:

Stamford Grand Adelaide

Glenelg, South Australia –

Accommodation in Adelaide to Enjoy the Countryside: McLaren Vale

If you are visiting South Australia specifically for the wine, you might want to consider lodging in McLaren Vale, which is a suburb of Adelaide.

Even though this unassuming community of fewer than 4,000 people is only about 40 kilometers south of Adelaide's downtown, staying here would make for a very different vacation.

In and around McLaren Vale, some of the oldest grapevines in the world continue to produce top-notch red wines. Explore the outdoors by taking a stroll along the Shiraz Trail.

Another popular event is the farmer's market on Saturday morning. If you decide to stay in the country, it will be simple to arrange a day trip to Adelaide because it is so close by, or vice versa.

Accommodations in McLaren Vale

Affordable lodging options in McLaren Vale:

The Linear Way Bed and Breakfast

Casa Swift

Friends at McLaren Vale

Mid-range accommodation in McLaren Vale:

SULTANA – Maximalist Accommodation

McLaren Vale Studio Apartments

Settlers Cottage

Bella Cosa Bed and Breakfast

Family – Friendly lodge in McLaren Vale:

Serafino McLaren Vale

McLaren Vale Motel & Apartments

3 Pears on the Park McLaren Vale

WayWood Wines Your Vineyard Getaway

Affordable Luxury Lodge in McLaren Vale:

Hotel California Road at Inkwell Wines

Beresford Estate

CABN Off-Grid Lux Cabins

McLaren Vale wine Valley -- at sunset South Australia

Accommodation in Adelaide to Enjoy Some Wine:
BAROSSA VALLEY

Wine aficionados also have the option of staying in the renowned Barossa Valley, which is a little further away from Adelaide.

Shiraz grapes are also well-known in this area, which is located around 75 kilometers northeast of Adelaide. There are many vineyards and tasting rooms in the local towns of Nuriootpa, Tanunda, and Angaston.

There are several luxurious lodging options in the Barossa Valley, making it the ideal destination for anyone searching for a luxurious break.

Caravans and vacation parks are only a few of the mid-range and low-cost lodging options available in the Barossa Valley.

Accommodations in the Barossa Valley

Low-cost lodging in the Barossa Valley:

Lyndoch Hill

Tanunda Cottages

Ambrosia Holiday Home

Lindsay House Homestead

Mid-range accommodation in Barossa Valley:

CABN CANVS Seppeltsfield

The Wine Vine Hotel

Stoneleigh Cottage Bed and Breakfast

Le Mas Barossa

Family-Friendly Accommodation in Barossa Valley:

Novotel Barossa Valley Resort

The Tanunda Club Guest Suites

The Clyde Greenock

Barossa Valley View Guesthouse

Affordable Luxury Lodge in Barossa Valley:

The Louise

The Residence at Barossa Chateau

Barossa Weintal Hotel

You can verify all the above accommodations in booking.com

Welcome To Australia

Conclusion

Australia is a stunning and diverse nation that provides a wide range of travel options for visitors of all ages and interests. In Australia, there is something to interest everyone, regardless of whether they are history buffs, environment lovers, or foodies.

We have examined many parts of Australia in this book, including its fascinating history, vibrant culture, and breathtaking natural vistas. We have supplied crucial travel information, such as details about money and currency, the weather and climate, and the best places to eat and drink in Australia. – **Chapter One as a Reference**

Various modes of transportation in Australia have also been discussed, including driving privately, taking trains, and using public transportation. We have highlighted the least expensive methods of getting across Australia for individuals on a tight budget. – **Chapter Two as a Reference**

This book goes into great detail about many types of lodging, such as hotels, resorts, cheap hotels, camping, and homestays. The top cheap hotels in Sydney, including those on the beach, in the city center, and close to Sydney Harbour, have been recommended by our team. – **Chapter Three as a Reference**

The principal locations covered in this book are Sydney, Melbourne, Brisbane, Perth, and Adelaide. Comprehensive information on each city's famous landmarks, attractions, outdoor activities, and experiences is included. We have also provided tips on Sydney's top attractions, restaurants, and beaches, as well as details on Melbourne's physical and demographic landscape. -- **From Chapters 4 through 8**

Along with information on their famous landmarks, tourist attractions, and outdoor activities, Brisbane and Perth are also highlighted. Chapter Six and Chapter Seven discuss Adelaide, including information on the city's well-known sights and lodging options in the Adelaide CBD, North Adelaide, Adelaide Hills, Glenelg Adelaide, McLaren Vale, and the Barossa Valley.

We hope that this book has given you the desire to discover all that Australia, a place of limitless opportunity, has to offer. Australia is undoubtedly a traveler's dream with its breathtaking natural scenery, dynamic towns, and extensive history. So prepare for the trip of a lifetime to Australia by packing your bags and cameras!

References

12 Best Things to Do in Melbourne - What is Melbourne Most Famous For? - Go Guides. (2023). Hotels.com. https://www.hotels.com/go/australia/things-to-do-melbourne

Growth Machine. (2023, February 28). *6 Memorable Facts About Australian Currency.* Beyond Borders. https://blog.remitly.com/currencies/australian-currency/

NomadicMatt. (2018, April 21). *How to Get Around Australia on the Cheap (UPDATED 2023).* Nomadic Matt's Travel Site. https://www.nomadicmatt.com/travel-blogs/how-to-get-around-oz-cheaply/

Rosen, E. (2022, March 11). *7 outdoor activities in Sydney perfect for travel during COVID-19 - The Points Guy.* The Points Guy. https://thepointsguy.com/guide/outdoor-activities-sydney-australia/

12 Top-Rated Attractions & Things to Do in Perth. (2023). Planetware.com. https://www.planetware.com/tourist-attractions-/perth-aus-wa-p.htm

Schultz, A. (2017). *12 Best Things to do in Adelaide, South Australia*. Touropia. https://www.touropia.com/tourist-attractions-in-adelaide/

Samantha. (2023, February 11). *Where to stay in Adelaide [Most Comprehensive Guide for 2023]*. Travelling King. https://www.travellingking.com/where-to-stay-in-adelaide/

10 Best Museums in Sydney - Where to Discover Sydney History, Art and Culture? - Go Guides. (2023). Hotels.com. https://www.hotels.com/go/australia/best-museums-sydney

10 Best Foods to Eat in Sydney - Real Aussie Dishes That Locals Love to Eat - Go Guides. (2023). Hotels.com. https://www.hotels.com/go/australia/best-foods-sydney

10 Best Beaches in Sydney - Which Sydney Beach is Right For You? - Go Guides. (2023). Hotels.com. https://www.hotels.com/go/australia/best-beaches-sydney

Perth | Western Australia, Australia | Britannica. (2023). In *Encyclopædia Britannica*.

https://www.britannica.com/place/Perth-Western-Australia

Melbourne | History, Population, Map, Climate, & Facts | Britannica. (2023). In *Encyclopædia Britannica*. https://www.britannica.com/place/Melbourne

Adelaide | South Australia, Australia | Britannica. (2023). In *Encyclopædia Britannica*. https://www.britannica.com/place/Adelaide

boukobza, sarah. (2022, November 19). *Migrating to Australia: Climate Zones and Weather*. Study Destination Australia; Study Destination Australia. https://studydestination.com.au/blogs/travel/migrating-to-australia-climate-zones-and-weather#:~:text=Summer%20is%20hot%20and%20dry,due%20to%20its%20tropical%20climate.

Scott, J. (2022, February 21). *36 Most Popular Australian Foods Visitors Have To Try In 2023*. Lacademie. https://www.lacademie.com/australian-foods/

The best luxury hotels in Australia – Tourism Australia. (2023, April 11). Australia.com.

https://www.australia.com/en/things-to-do/luxury/best-luxury-hotels-australia.html

https://www.facebook.com/paula.morgan. (2023, January 24). *How to find a good budget-priced hotel in Sydney.* Sydney Travel Guide. https://sydneyexpert.com/budget-hotels-sydney/

Editor. (2019, February 3). *The Best Caravan Parks In Australia By State.* Australian Traveller. https://www.australiantraveller.com/australia/australias-best-caravan-parks/

THE BEST Farm Stays: Australia (2023) - Farm Stay Planet. (2023). Farm Stay Planet. https://www.farmstayplanet.com/farmstays/australia-1/

Brisbane Introduction Walking Tour. (2023). GPSmyCity. https://www.gpsmycity.com/tours/brisbane-introduction-walking-tour-3186.html

Schultz, A. (2017). *12 Top Tourist Attractions in Brisbane, Australia.* Touropia. https://www.touropia.com/tourist-attractions-in-brisbane-australia/

Dreghorn, B. (2018, March 26). *11 outdoor activities near Brisbane City - Student One*. Student One. https://studentone.com/10-outdoor-activities-near-brisbane-city/

Sydney - New World Encyclopedia. (2023). Newworldencyclopedia.org. https://www.newworldencyclopedia.org/entry/Sydney

(2023). Local-Insider.com. https://local-insider.com/post/top-30-places-to-visit-in-sydney-landmarks-that-will-wow-you-for-sure/61334375afccd60a0bfca289

22529085R00181